IN SPITE OF

DAVID MINOR

ISBN 979-8-88540-306-1 (paperback)
ISBN 979-8-88540-307-8 (digital)

Christian Faith Publishing
832 Park Avenue
Meadville, PA 16335
www.christianfaithpublishing.com

Printed in the United States of America

To Michele, who encouraged me many times to write my story.

I wrote this book during the coronavirus outbreak when we were sheltered in place. "Remember? This is a perfect time," she said. I am not grateful for the pandemic, but I am grateful that I had the time.

For the four weeks I was furloughed, I spent every morning alone with nature in the park next door to our subdivision, writing.

I also want to dedicate this book to my children—Jesse, Lauren, and Jennifer.

Also to my dear mother, Lorraine Minor.

I love you all.

ACKNOWLEDGMENTS

Without the many I need to mention, none of what you will read would have ever happened. To my grandparents, especially my grandmother and her example of love for all. To my mother, who I had to share with many, but her heart was big enough for all. I cannot count the number of people she fed at her table. To my father and his example to have a vision and believe without wavering until he saw it came to pass. To the beautiful congregation of the Gospel Tabernacle, who supported me faithfully, and the countless numbers who traveled with me so many times to Romania. I would love to write all of their names, but I am afraid I would miss one, so please forgive me.

To the many businesses that donated and helped with medications and supplies. To the building teams and those that helped with the youth mission trips. To Jason Holmberg, who was so faithful to continue the work in Romania. To Michele, who has been the greatest encourager to me to tell my story. And to my three children, Jesse, Lauren, and Jennifer, who were willing to share their dad with others.

I also want to dedicate this book to my wonderful brothers and sisters. Sharon, my loving older sister; Karen, my second sister, a wonderful person; my brother, Timothy, my younger brother who was a faithful pastor and passed away a few years ago. To my brother Judge Stephen Minor, who has been a blessing to many; and my brother Pastor John Minor, who now is pastoring the Gospel Tabernacle in Pennsylvania, a wonderful, faithful man. Lastly, and again so important, is my mother, one of those of whom the world is not worthy.

INTRODUCTION

I am standing in a large field with a small concrete building in the center. "You must see this," our guide proclaimed. Following him, I entered through the small door and was shocked to find a concrete table with some kind of tie-downs attached to it. In an almost non-chalant way and broken English, our guide proclaimed, "Many lost lives here. This is the place where Christians and political prisoners were tortured." He explained that many of them who had died were buried in the field that surrounded the building.

The table was still stained with blood from the poor souls that were the victims of such a bloody dictator until a few months ago. To myself, I thought, *This is what a godforsaken country looks like, and how grateful I am that I live in America.*

Stepping outside to breathe, my mind could not stop playing the image of the inside of that room. I began to push the semi-frozen dirt aside with my shoe. To my shock and horror, a human bone began to appear. *I cannot wait to leave this dark place and never return,* I thought. Little did I know this place of great suffering and sorrow would become part of my life story. Also, I came to understand, as I hope you do, when you do good to those who can do you no good in return, God does for you what you cannot do for yourself.

CHAPTER 1

Chaos and Danger, Sounds Like Fun

Come with me to Romania. Why not? Pastor Jim Finn was the Indiana Jones of evangelists. Traveling around the world, smuggling Bibles into communist countries, he also had a great ministry for healing the sick. *This could be quite the trip*, I thought. He had previously traveled to Romania and had some contacts with both the underground churches and the so-called free churches that quickly began to spring up after the fall of the dictator Nicolae Ceausescu. It was now the early '90s, just after the revolution had ended, which culminated with the dictator and his wife's execution on Christmas Day 1989. The country was still in chaos, but Jim assured me we would be okay, so we booked the trip.

Flying from New York to Munich, then renting a car, we drove through Germany into Austria, then Hungary. It was quite a breathtaking trip. I noticed Hungary seemed a bit run-down, but nothing compared to when we crossed the border and were admitted into Romania. It was like walking back in time. Literally everything was broken. Streetlights, red lights, bridges, highways—everything was in such disrepair. Beyond all of this, what consumed me was the overwhelming spirit of hopelessness.

I remembered visiting Haiti years ago and seeing the poverty there, but it was nothing compared to Romania's despair and darkness. Home seemed like heaven in comparison to this. As we drove further into the country, I knew this would be my last mission trip. We arrived in Timisoara in the darkness of night and were able to find a phone to call the host pastor. I was never so happy to see him! We followed him to his home and greeted his wife. Exhausted, I could not wait for sleep and home.

C H A P T E R   2

Grandmother Diagnosed with Religious Hysteria?

My grandmother, Sophia Minor, was one of the most loving yet unique people you would ever meet. She was born in Tennessee. She had red hair and a very quick tongue. Grandma was raised with a bit of prejudice and never associated much with Black people. My grandparents married at a very young age. She was fifteen years old, and he was a couple of years older. They eloped in the next county over. They had met at the local store that was owned by his father.

A few years after they were married, my grandfather was hired and trained as a detective with a company that worked for the transit system in different cities. It was a private company with contracts with many cities. He would go from city to city, undercover, and investigate theft among the drivers of the buses. During the Depression, my grandparents first lived in Buffalo, and they got by like everyone else did at the time. At some point, my grandmother began attending a church. My aunt told me of how upset she was because they wanted her to take her earrings off. "What does God care about my earrings?" she said. She didn't like all of their rules and regulations. She never talked much about church after that.

After a few years, they moved to Brooklyn. I remember growing up listening to my grandfather talk about the many stories of when he was a detective. Although he had a badge and a gun, I am sure he was never involved in any real danger. They had two sons and one daughter at the time—my father, David; his older brother, James; and his sister, Dorothy. When the Japanese bombed Pearl Harbor, every young man that was of age signed up for military duty. My uncle did the same, joining the Marines. He was sent to Paris Island Marine boot camp. One thing for sure, her son was not going off to war. She wrote a letter to the president that, by some way, he actually read.

She stated that her son was sickly and could not go to war. My Uncle Jim was called into the drill sergeant's office one morning. "Son, I have a letter from your mother to the president of the United States. He has read this letter, and according to your mother, you are sickly. Is this true?"

"No, I am fine," my uncle stated. With that, he was sent back to his platoon. My grandmother was so upset. She had no idea what to do. She got to the president, but it didn't help.

One morning, on the way to the store, my grandmother passed by a storefront church. The door was open, and she heard women praying rather loudly. She peered into the door and saw around twenty Black ladies, all praying together. Being from the South, and raised with some prejudice, she immediately backed away. One of the ladies noticed her and said, "Can I help you?"

In her Southern drawl, Grandma asked, "What are y'all doing?"

The lady opened a little book. In this book were many names of boys. "These boys are all going to war," she said, "and we pray until God says they will come home alive."

Now this was something that got Grandma's attention. She was all in. For the first time in her life, she walked into a room being the only White and had her life-changing experience.

She returned home, and when my grandfather heard this glorious news, he went ballistic. "You were where? They told you what? You have lost your mind!" He even called the doctor, telling him that his wife had gone crazy. "She is spending the day with—" I won't use the words he used. "I need to have her committed."

The doctor told my grandfather that my grandmother had "religious hysteria." He said it was common with mothers who have sons going off to war. His advice was that she would get over it. Every day, against my grandfather's wishes and prejudice, my grandmother went to the little storefront church and prayed with the Black ladies.

It must have been a sight—one red-haired lady from Tennessee, and the rest all Black.

The battleship *Missouri* was built in the Brooklyn Naval Yard. It was to be the greatest ship America had ever made. My uncle was to be on this ship. It would sail from New York to Virginia Beach for the outfitting of the guns. Then it would be sent to the Pacific to fight the Japanese. It was called the Mighty Mo. My uncle was now back from Paris Island, waiting at home for orders to sail.

Every day, Grandma prayed with the Black ladies while my grandfather ridiculed her. She told my uncle, "That boat will not leave the harbor until God tells me you're coming home safe."

"Are you crazy, woman?" my grandfather screamed. "You are not dealing with those crazy people at your stupid church. You're dealing with the United States Government. When they say the boat sails, the boat sails."

One evening, Uncle Jim got the orders he was to leave in the morning. He got up and packed his duffel bag, ate breakfast, and said, "Kiss me goodbye, Mamma."

"I will not," she said. "The boat cannot leave until I hear from God that you will come home."

My grandfather screamed at her, but she would not relent. No kiss.

That evening, as she made dinner, she set a place for Uncle Jim. As they were sitting down for dinner, he walked in. "There was a problem with the boat," he said, "and it could not sail."

Without a word, my grandma said, "Come eat your dinner."

The next morning, the same exact thing. "Not until I hear from God," she said.

And that evening, he was back. They had somehow gotten stuck in shallow water. The third day, the exact same scenario, and dinner was served. That night, Grandma had her visitation from God. He promised her that Jimmy would return safely. In the morning, she kissed him goodbye.

A few weeks later, while lying on her bed, my grandfather walked into her room and threw the *New York Times* on my grandmother's bed. "Read it," he said. "Front page. 'Japanese Sink the Missouri!'

There is your God, you stupid woman. Now get your black dress on, we are going to mourn."

My grandmother rose and told him, "Get that piece of s—t off my bed. It is a lie!" She never allowed any of this to sway her faith from what God said to her. Turns out, the paper got it wrong. My grandmother got it right—fake news.

My uncle returned safely but had many stories of how the Japanese tried, for three days, to sink the *Missouri*. They sent kamikaze pilots with planes loaded with explosives with just enough fuel to reach the ships. He had pictures of one that crashed into the *Missouri*, just a few feet from where he was, but for some unknown reason, it never exploded! However, my uncle got a small piece of shrapnel stuck in his back. The fire that ensued was quickly put out. The only death that occurred on the *Missouri* was the kamikaze pilot. God protected that whole ship.

That was the beginning of my grandmother's incredible spiritual journey. She really did not like organized religion but loved people, any color, any race. All were welcomed by Grandma.

CHAPTER 3

Why Me?

In 1954, my grandmother moved to Coudersport, Pennsylvania, along with my grandfather. According to her, God told her to begin a church there that would touch the nations. My aunt said that she had looked for the location for five years. She drove all over three states, looking for this special place. They found a *Stroud Real Estate* magazine with properties from all over the United States in it. While flipping through the pages, they saw a property that looked promising, so they took a trip to Pennsylvania. They booked a little cottage right outside of a town called Coudersport. That night, she had another of her amazing visitations. She awoke and announced to my grandfather, "This is the place."

Over the years, numerous guests, some of them with great problems, all found their way to her home to experience love and compassion. In 1956, my family moved to Coudersport to join my grandmother and grandfather. At that time, I had two older sisters, Karen and Sharon. My grandmother started having church in their living room. The grand total of the church was my family, my grandparents, the town drunk, and my grandmother's hairdresser.

There was quite a bit of prejudice against my family because we were from Long Island, and my father found it near impossible to find work. We were living in my grandmother's home that had many problems. For one, the well was polluted. For years, I would take my little red wagon with one-gallon glass jars to get water from the neighbors. Many of the neighbors would ask me to quit coming, and I would have to find another home. My father's pride would not allow him to pick up the surplus food the government gave away, but the people who did get it would drop what they did not want to our house. How I hated that Spam! I remember, one Thanksgiving, Spam was our turkey. My dad actually put cloves on it, poured pancake syrup on top of it, and baked it in the oven. He didn't fool us; it wasn't ham either. I was sure I did not want to be some poor pastor after living like this. Sad to admit, I did not want to even be a Christian.

We grew up very strict. Everything was a sin—the movies, the prom, television, you name it. If it was fun, then it was a sin. So as a young boy, I was so envious of those that had more. Along with the ridiculous prejudice, I pretty much had made up my mind that none of this was for me. The only thing I was allowed to do was sports, but I was a skinny little kid and did not excel. I remember going out for track when I was fifteen years old. Mr. Kirby was our coach and also our biology teacher. I had no idea what sport I wanted to do, so for some stupid reason, I said, "I want to run distance."

What that meant was that they took me, along with a bunch of real athletes, seven miles out of town and said, "Run back to the school."

The athletes quickly ran on ahead of me until they were out of sight. I ran about a hundred yards and collapsed along the road. I just was not cut out for this. My side hurt, my head hurt, and my feet hurt. After about an hour, I hitchhiked the rest of the way back. I actually arrived shortly after the athletes, so Mr. Kirby probably thought I would do okay. Sometimes we would have to run around the town or up a hill. I hated it but did not want to quit.

The day of the first track meet came, and Mr. Kirby had me entered in the two-mile relay. If I remember correctly, I had to run two times around the track, which equaled half of a mile. I was the third leg, and the athletes before me had gotten us a great lead. When it came to my turn, I took off strong but soon was falling behind. My father was in the crowd and was asked by the lady beside him, "Do you know who that kid is that's running so slow?"

"No," he said. This went on for the next few track meets. Mr. Kirby would put me in, and I would lose the race for the rest of the guys. I guess they had enough and made up a story that I was smoking. This would mean I would be put off the track team. He brought me into his office before practice and asked me if it was true. "No," I told him. "It is not." I believed he knew I was telling the truth.

Then Mr. Kirby said something to me that I have never forgotten. "David, if I could pick one person from this whole school to be on my team and only one, that would be you." I will never forget his words and the time he took to make me feel important. He was much more than a teacher or coach; he was a great example of a caring human being.

My best friend was also my cousin, Jim Minor Jr., and we were fifteen and sixteen years old when my grandmother called us to her home for a talk. I will never forget sitting on her bed as she said these words to us: "Both of you boys are called to love people. You are called to help the desperate, and you are called to be in ministry." This was the last thing I wanted to hear. Then she went on to say that she had dreamed last night of two young men in caskets. You guessed it. It was us. For two weeks, I did my best to convince myself that Grandma had been eating something that gave her a nightmare.

Three weeks later, my cousin and I were picked up by a friend, Micky Lambert, who had the fastest car in town. I had seen the speedometer pass 135 mph, many times. As we left the red light, behind us appeared a car that challenged our driver to a race. Suddenly, we are racing down busy Main Street, Route 6, on a Saturday afternoon. We passed the jail, passed the car dealer, passed the churches, faster and faster with blind curves. For over two miles, we raced on the wrong side of the road at speeds over one hundred miles per hour.

In my mind, I could hear my grandmother's words. In the back of that car, on the floorboard, Jimmy and I were eyeball to eyeball, literally crying tears of fear. We prayed. I could see the casket my grandmother had described. This moment I will never forget. "Get us out of this alive, and we will do anything, even become pastors." It was, for me, one of the most fearful times of my life. I knew we were going to die. I could literally smell the breath of death. But God stopped traffic and spared our lives. We finally passed the car we were racing, just missing a head-on collision with a car coming in the other direction. Who was in that car? My grandparents.

Reluctantly, a few years later, I enrolled in a school of ministry, graduated, returned home, and married. Our church was few in numbers, perhaps fifty strong, and it was barely able to support my father. I still had no great interest in being a pastor, so I looked for a job. What kind of job can you get with a degree in ministry? None. I was desperate to work, and a friend of mine had a disposal business. Yes, he was the garbage man. "Would you like to drive the garbage truck?" he asked.

"Not really," I said. But I had no other options, so I accepted the lofty position. Quite a blow to my pride, I disguised myself with a baseball hat and sunglasses. I wondered if this is what I was going to do until, someday, the church grew larger.

My father prayed about it, came to me, and said "David, God is going to give you a job, somehow, in government. You should begin to look for that."

A new neighbor had moved next door to our home. One evening, he explained he was working for a private appraisal company who had a contract with our local county to appraise all the taxable property of the county. This would last about two years. He also said they were hiring one more person to do the appraisals. I went for the interview but was told no because my ministry schooling had absolutely nothing to do with real estate. I thought for sure this was the job my dad had told me about. When I told him they said no, he said, "Go back again."

I did reluctantly. What did I have to lose?

The office was located in the basement of the local courthouse. There was a side entrance where you can go directly into the basement. I walked down the hall, his door was open, and he waved me in. This time, Rick was on the phone, talking to someone. He said to him, "I got a guy I can hire today, but his schooling is in ministry. Okay." He hung up the phone, looked at me and said, "You're hired!"

Overnight, I went from a garbage truck driver to county appraiser. I went through the training and was soon on my own, doing a great job and enjoying it. I worked for a year, and then the company got a contract for the next county over, so I continued with them.

One Monday morning, a supervisor, Dennis, who none of us had met before, was at our meeting. He did commercial appraising, and he also, for some reason, hated me. He would ridicule everything I said or did. All of a sudden, I was wrong. Have you ever hated a job? I mean from loving to hating? I would dread going in every morning and dealing with this miserable person. He told one of my friends that he was going to get me fired. "I have done it before," he gloated. This went on for about three weeks, and I could not bear it anymore. Why would God give me such a great job to then give me this idiot to deal with?

I will never forget the day Marvin, one the owners, showed up on a Monday morning. "I want to work with all the residential appraisers," he said. "I am going to start with David Minor."

I thought, *This is it. I am being fired today.* We got into my car and headed for the area that I would be working in.

"What are you all about, Minor?" Marvin asked me.

I began to tell him of my grandmother and our little church and that someday, I would be in ministry. With that, he began to confide in me a personal matter. It was a heartbreaking experience he was going through and needed someone to help him. We spent the next three days together while everyone wondered what was going on.

On Wednesday night, Marvin came with me to our little basement church, and we prayed together. I can only say that Marvin was a very grateful man.

That evening, Marvin came to my house with a gift for my newborn daughter, Jennifer. He was so happy.

The next morning, coming into work, he met me at the door with a great hug. "I am going home," he said. "But before I do, is there anything in the world I can do for you?"

"Hmmm, well, there is one little thing." I told him about Dennis and his treatment of me.

With a look of great anger, he said, "David, you go to work, I will take care of this." I was told later how Marvin looked for Dennis, who was not working where he was supposed to be, the commercial area of Bradford, Pennsylvania. Instead, Marvin found him at the YMCA, swimming. He fired him right in the middle of his backstroke!

A few years later, the company was finished in the area. I did not want to move away, so I answered an ad for an electrical distributor salesperson. The company was only a year old with a rented warehouse and rented vehicles. The owner laughed at my resume but liked me and said, "Let's give it a try." His name was Tom Hall, and we would become lifelong friends.

A few months after starting my new job, our little church in Coudersport bought ten acres of land on Route 6. I will tell you about this land in the next few chapters, but it was a perfect place to build my grandmother's, and now my father's, vision for our town.

My Father's Faith

My father never seemed to get discouraged. I really can remember very few times when life would get him down. He would often speak of all the great things that were going to take place. Yes, he had great faith but very little money. As I've mentioned, for years, the church consisted of a few people in the basement of his home, all poor, the most rejected in our town. My father had helped many people over the years, one being John Geminez.

John was a hopeless heroin addict, which lead to a life of crime. He had done time at every major prison in New York. Many had tried to help him, but he could never break away from his habit. Faith and love were the only rehabs my father could offer. Giving him another chance, where many had given up, he came to live in our home, and we called him Uncle John. He became a part of our family. John broke out of the chains of addiction. He became a man of faith. He changed the way he looked at God, looked at life. He wanted to help others do the same. Two things I loved about Uncle John were his rice and beans and his great voice. I enjoyed them simultaneously. I remember waking up in the morning, a few times, to the aroma of rice and beans along with him singing.

Uncle John married his sweetheart, Ann, and in a few years, they moved to Virginia, where John started a church in Virginia Beach. It was called Rock Church. From a few people in a living room, Rock Church grew into thousands of members, one of the largest churches in Virginia Beach. John was very grateful to my father and wanted to do something to thank him. My dad had an old station wagon that needed to retire. John asked him to come to Virginia Beach to speak at the church at their anniversary celebration.

While he was there, he was presented with a brand-new Lincoln automobile. "This is for you, Pastor, my gift to you." He loved my father dearly. What did Dad do? Brought it home, put it in the paper, and sold it. Then he put the money in the building fund for the church that he wanted to build someday. This happened twice to my father, where people bought him cars. The second time, it was again a brand-new Lincoln.

My father did the exact same thing and put the money into the building fund. His dream and vision were all that mattered to him. My father was never wealthy, even when the church grew. His joy and fulfillment were found in changing the hearts of people and seeing them succeed in life. He never let his lack or his setbacks ever deter what he knew was going to happen. He did not have wealth, but he had vision and faith. I learned from him what true wealth really means. He was the example of living by faith, not sight. He truly embraced the teaching of Jesus when He calmed the disciples' fears about tomorrow. "What will we eat? What will we wear? Where will we live?" Like you and me, security is what they wanted. Just to know that all their needs would be met, He answered, "Don't worry about tomorrow. Live in this day." Faith lives today as if all will be well tomorrow because it *will* be well. This is what I learned from my father.

I want to tell how we acquired the property to build the church on. My father loved this piece of property. It was part of a large estate with a beautiful home owned by a local doctor. My father had approached the man, kindly asking if he could purchase the land to build his church there. It was an emphatic "*no*." In fact, the man was not too friendly to the idea at all. "Over my dead body will you ever build a church there!"

I remember my father taking me out to the land after the man had said no. "Here, we will build a church, a gymnasium, a children's church, dining halls, and a senior retirement community center, and then a second larger church, someday, when we grow," he said. I thought he was delusional.

First of all, we had, maybe, fifty people, all of them broke! There were only two thousand people in our town and only fifteen thousand in our whole county. We had one red light in the whole county. I said to myself and then to him, "Didn't that man tell you no?"

"Yes, he did. But my faith is bigger than that. I choose to believe. This is not about him. This is about faith. This is my dream, and I am making plans for it because it *will* happen." Well, bless his heart, shortly after this conversation, the man that owned the property died. We did not rejoice. The estate was bought by a local attorney who was more than happy to sell the land to the church. My father taught me a huge lesson here. Faith is powerful. Faith looks forward at what will be and celebrates it, talks about it, feels it, and becomes it.

The congregation, though small in number, broke ground and began to build the church. The building would seat five hundred people. In the basement would be a dining room, classrooms, and offices. It took all we had. After a few months of free sweat and labor, the foundation was done, the floor was on the foundation, and the walls were on the outside of the building. It was the morning for the trusses to be raised. I remember leaving for work that morning. I would drive by the new church being built and would always think of those words, "Over his dead body!" Not that I ever wished him harm, but the timing was most interesting.

It was a Wednesday, a typical day. I went into the office, called the electrical contractors I would be visiting that day, chatted with Tom for a few minutes, then off to see my customers. Around 6:00 p.m., I started the trip back to my home. As I was driving down Route 6, I could not wait to see how the building would look with the new trusses. When I got there, I was shocked at what I saw. The building was gone! Yes, gone! I drove into the parking lot, exited my car, and ran to where it was. It had totally collapsed.

I found out later that after all the trusses were on the wall, someone climbed up to move the end truss, something he should not have done. When he tried to move the one truss, it fell into the next one, causing a domino effect, bringing all of them crashing to the floor. When they hit the floor, it gave way, and the total structure ended up in the basement, a twisted mess of lumber. When I saw this, I thought, *My God, maybe it just happened, and no one knows, or worse, maybe someone died here.*

I rushed to my father's house, flying through the front door, bounded upstairs to his bedroom. He was in the shower, singing some joyful gospel song. *He doesn't know*, I thought. "Dad, Dad, the church has fallen down."

"Yes," he said joyfully, "but no one was hurt. Quite a miracle!" If truly there was a man who could find the silver lining, it was him. It sure was a miracle no one died or was injured, as at least twelve men were working in the building when it came down. Now for me, if I were him, I would not have had this positive attitude. He taught me a big lesson here. "All is well," he said, "and I believe we're going to build even faster than we were, and we are going to have some help from many businesses." One thing for sure, everyone knew about it. It was in all the local papers.

Well, we started again. Cleaning up took at least a week, but in about three weeks, we were ready for the new trusses. The truss company felt great compassion for us and did not charge us again. *Wow,* I thought as I thanked the man, *perhaps my dad was right.* God put favor in the heart of local businessmen to have compassion for us.

"Dave, can you find us a crane?" my dad asked.

"I am sure I can, but do you have the money to pay?"

"No," he said. "We are out of money, just ask him to give it to us."

"Really?" I had a contractor friend in St Mary's, Pennsylvania, who I was seeing that day. "Do you know anyone with a crane?" I asked him.

He had already read about the building falling down, so he was aware. "I do know a guy, but I am pretty sure he will make you pay full price. He is a tough businessman."

Well, I drove over to his company and asked to see him. I told him who I was and that I had come on behalf of the church to see if we could use his crane. I will never forget, the price was fifty-two bucks an hour, his words. "It's the same price for everyone," he said, quite emphatically. So I took a three-point shot.

At the present time, the economy in the area was not too good. I quoted him a scripture from the Old Testament, "If you bless my people, I will bless you." I told him, "God can pay way better than the $52 per hour."

He looked at me and said, "Okay, you can have the crane."

I was so surprised that he said yes. Another act of kindness.

He said, "Please pay for the fuel and pay the operator."

"Of course," I said, "no problem. Thank you so much."

A few days later, the job was done, the trusses were up, and the operator was so blessed to be around such amazing people. He *also* refused to be paid. I wondered to myself how God would repay these people for their kindness and compassion. We certainly could not afford to do it.

Since that worked out so well, I went to a bunch of local businesses, since they had all read about the church collapse, to ask for help. The tile company gave me tile, the glass block company gave me glass blocks, and the initial 400-amp three-phase service into the building was donated. It was quite amazing, and I am convinced that if the building had not fallen down, we would never have been able to do it on our own. Good things can come out of bad circumstances if you remain in faith.

We came to the place where we needed all the electrical for the inside. Wire, conduit, boxes, subpanels, fans, and very expensive church-type lighting. Now it is one thing to walk into a stranger's office and ask for free stuff. If they say no, you walk away, all good. But now I needed electrical supplies from a man who I had not worked that long for. I knew he liked me, but I also knew that even if he was willing, he could not afford to make this type of donation.

I went into his office, shut the door and, as gently as I could, told him of our needs. "Dave, I have been thinking about this, and I want to give you everything at cost. I will not make a penny."

Sounded good to me, and so nice of him, but since we didn't have *any* money, that was not going to work. So I explained how God blesses you when you bless his people.

"You want me to give it to you?" he asked.

"Yes," I said. And for some reason, he did. I remember bringing a truck home that night, loaded with all we needed. The rest would ship directly from the factories. My father was overjoyed, but I was still nervous. What if it doesn't work, and this poor guy goes broke listening to me? I didn't have the faith yet that my father did.

In the morning, I got in early to work, about 7:30. Tom was in his office, on the phone, and other lines were ringing. I put down my briefcase and answered it. "Electrical Products Unlimited," I said.

"Good morning, this is T. H. Green Electric. Do you have five hundred feet of 350 Copper THW?"

"Yes," I said.

"Well, can you send it on the next truck?" And this continued one after the other, people calling in orders. After about twenty minutes of this, nonstop, we caught a break, and I walked into his office.

"Dave," he said, "the strangest thing, these people are calling in with orders who have never bought from us before."

God was doing his part for Tom. When he gave to those who could do no good in return, God did for him what he could not do for himself. Within a few years, we were one of the largest distributors in the state, loved by our contractors but hated by our competition.

I also had a conversation with my contractor friend who sent me to the man with the crane. He told me how that man had received a very large contract to build a large building for a local factory after having given me the crane. In the middle of a poor economy, he was awarded the contract without having to bid. He gave us a crane for two days and lost $52 for sixteen hours of work. God gave him a factory to build over the next year. I am sure it paid fifty-two bucks for many, many hours!

As for me, after a few years, I decided to start my own business, a wholesale tire and auto parts store. I also bought many apartment buildings and built and sold spec homes. I was very successful, lived in a big house on a mountain, and was so happy to have accomplished the American dream. I was not living the life I did as a young boy. We were not poor, and it was quite enjoyable. I had a gentleman's farm with horses and sheep that my children would show at the local fair. It was a wonderful time raising them, and I loved every moment. It was then that I got that call.

I was thirty-five years old when my father suffered his first heart attack. Now he needed me. It was then I kept my part of the bargain to become a pastor. I sold my business, and overnight, was in ministry. I was back to making $25,000 per year. I moved out of the house on the mountain and bought a more modest home in town. I made the best of it. Our church grew and grew until we became the largest church in the community. We produced a local television program called *Good News*, built a retirement home for our elderly, gymnasium for the youth, dining hall, and a children's church. I was very comfortable, and then Pastor Jim Finn said, "Come to Romania with me."

CHAPTER 5

The Bloody Revolution!

From 1948 to 1989, Romania was communist. The dictator, Nicolae Ceausescu, was an evil man. Most of the food that was produced by the farmers in Romania was shipped to Russia. This was the agreement Ceausescu had with Moscow. They would prop him up, and he would send them food. The infrastructure of the country had collapsed while he lived in great luxury. Torture and killing was the consequence to any who spoke out against the communist dictator. If you would like to read the story of one pastor, it is titled *In God's Underground* by Richard Wurmbrand. I would highly recommend it. Sadly, he was tortured and beaten and imprisoned for fourteen years. It was horrible.

In Romania, God was dead. Breadlines and orphans were everywhere. Birth control was forbidden, and children were abandoned in hospitals and on the streets. At times, after two years of age, they were dumped into state orphanages under horrible conditions. At eighteen, they were released to their own demise. The dictator's sons were also horrible criminals with fearful reputations. The dictator had built the "People's House," a lavish building, actually the largest single structure in the world. It cost millions and millions of dollars while his people starved. An incredible waste of money. His secret police were everywhere, and people would be rounded up and taken away, never to return.

As the world began to change, and many communist regimes began to fall, the Romanian students began to protest. These protests began in Timisoara. It was the fall of 1989. Every day, the students would march to the headquarters of the secret police. There, they would be met by the army. Those who were near the front of the protest would die. Every day, they marched, and on our Thanksgiving Day of 1989, on a cold winter day, it all changed.

On this day, the army did not fire into the crowd. As the students chanted, "We are your brothers, we are your sisters," the army raised their weapons toward the building of the secret police and fired into the building. On Christmas Day, the dictator and his wife were executed, and a new government was formed. The problem would be that many of these people in the new government were corrupt, and it was a most dangerous place, still in chaos.

CHAPTER 6

Faces You Can't Forget

We visited many places. The stone building and mass graveyard I described at the beginning of the book, the birthplace of the revolution, the place where so many students were slaughtered as well as a cemetery where many of them were laid to rest. All during our visit, I saw so many children in the streets, many of them inhaling bags of glue, trying to escape their miserable lives. They were just children, four and five years old. The people walked by like it was nothing, just another day in Romania. Those faces, I could not forget. There was darkness and despair everywhere.

Somehow, we came upon the city dump, which was near a place we were visiting. What I saw there haunted me for a very long time— little children eating out of the dump. Beside them, rats scurried around, so sad and so profound. My time spent in Romania was one after the other, stories of abuse, persecution, and suffering. Again, godforsaken seemed the only way to describe this place. I was so happy when the trip ended, and we headed back to Munich for the trip home.

CHAPTER 7

No Sleep for You

*H*appy to be home, I tried to go back to my routine of ministry. Many people wanted to know about my trip, of course, and I shared with them all that I had witnessed. Here in America, we have poor, for sure, but nothing in comparison to what I saw in Romania. Every week, in our local community, where I live now, there are numerous sources for free and very good food. There are shelters available, and you would never see a child alone in the streets. But in Romania, it was common. I could not get the faces of the children out of my mind. Seeing it in a movie or even pictures from the newspaper is not the same as an eyewitness.

The smell, the rawness, and seeing this up close was profound. Even when I came home, days later, I could still smell Romania! What if I can do something? What if we can do something? I began to imagine building an orphanage or perhaps an international adoption agency or a way to bring medicine to the suffering children or even building a church. That would be cool! But where to start? What about the thousands of dollars it would take? That actually would be the easy part. The harder part was hearing this little voice that said, "You are totally incapable." This is the same voice that talks to you, and it was my biggest problem. Perhaps when you do good for those who cannot do good to us in return, God will do for us what we cannot do for ourselves, all in spite of me! Maybe in spite of you!

C H A P T E R   8

Let's Go Again

So the man who said he would never go again cannot sleep. I knew I should do something, but I felt the least qualified as well as not financially able to do what was in my heart and dream. Our church was the largest in town but nothing in comparison to the huge ministries that undertook building churches, orphanages, shipping vast amounts of medicine, or starting an international adoption agency. This is a job for a Joel Osteen or a Billy Graham.

What the world really needs are people who are willing, in spite of their lack, the place where the God factor is involved. This place is called the realm of miracles. If your own abilities were enough, you would never see the miraculous.

Knowing I had to return, Pastor Jim Finn and I decided to go again. Upon doing some research, we found we could fly to Budapest, Hungary, rent a car, and drive to Romania. Delta Airlines had a flight, so we booked it along with a rental car. We had made contact on our first trip with a pastor in a small free church in the town of Lipova. It was from there we would see the beginning of our Romanian journey. For me, two things I wanted to know simply were, one, what were their greatest needs? And two, how I can help?

The pastor had found a piece of land that was once a pig farm. Here, he expressed, we could build a church and an orphanage. Let's do the orphanage first, we agreed.

Returning to America, I began to share my stories of the great need in Romania. I shared with my church and local businesses my vision to remodel the old pig farm into an orphanage. The money was raised and sent to Romania, where the Romanian builders spent around six months to remodel the building. With the paperwork completed, we were approved in Romania to begin receiving the children from the state orphanages and loving them back to life. It is called Haven of Hope. Over twenty years later, many children have found a home at the Haven of Hope. Later I will tell you the stories of some of these children. They are loved and cared for by Pastor Moses Pop and his wife, Nutzi.

C H A P T E R   9

Can't Speak Romanian

$\mathcal{F}$or the first three or four trips to Romania, we used a local interpreter, a professor, from a school in Lipova. I knew it was not going to work with him very long because he was unreliable due to inebriation. He would also run on and on with his own advice, which was total nonsense. I realized, for me to accomplish what I needed to do there, I would need an interpreter that I could trust. If I could find an interpreter in America, it would be much better. I had been given the name of a young man living in Williamsport, Pennsylvania. His name was Valeriu Borlovan. His story was quite amazing, and I would like to share it with you.

In 1988, Val was eighteen years old and was living in Romania. Many would try to escape the horribleness of this dictator. The borders were well-guarded, and being caught meant prison, hard labor, or worse. Val had met a man who worked in Timisoara but lived in a small village, Dudestii Vechi, near to the Yugoslavia border. Val and his boyhood friend were planning an escape. This gentleman promised them that they could come with him on the train to his village, then they would try to escape into Yugoslavia. If caught, they would face severe punishment.

On the day agreed, the man told Val that he was not going home that evening, but they would have to try another time. Val had already made up his mind to leave that evening, so he boarded the train along with his friend anyway. They knew they had to make a stop halfway to change trains. As they approached the train station, they saw many soldiers and police looking at the papers of the many

26

passengers. "We were never so afraid," Val explained to me. All of a sudden, they saw the man who was not going home on the same train they were on. He had lied to them, perhaps out of fear of the consequences. "You must help us," Val said.

"Follow me," he said. "I will help you get on the right train."

Jumping off the wrong side, they disembarked and followed him to another train. As they were getting settled, the man said, "I must use the restroom." Val did not trust him and followed him as he jumped off the train and headed to another. He had put them on a train going back to Timisoara. The train was leaving the station, so with no other choice, they both jumped off the train and ran to the train that the man had boarded. When the police came through the train, Val and his friend, both praying, acted asleep, and the police walked by without noticing, and soon they were on the way to the village near the border.

They arrived in the dark of night and, with great care, made their way into the forest that stood between them and freedom. If caught, Val knew he would go to prison. This is exactly what happened a few days into the journey. Val and his friend were caught and arrested. They spent thirty days in a prison in Belgrade. Would he be sent back? Or would he be free? It was totally in the hands of Yugoslavia.

The UN had a refugee camp outside of the city. Here, Val was sent, and he was allowed to seek asylum in many countries. The United States was his first choice. To come to America, he had to have a sponsor. His uncle lived in Germany and owned a small auto shop near the US Army base. He worked on the personal vehicle of one of the soldiers. That soldier had a cousin living in Pennsylvania who agreed to sponsor Val. I believe God knew that Val had to get to Pennsylvania for me so he could be my interpreter!

After thirty days of prison and six months in the refugee camp, Val was put on a plane to JFK. Attending school in Pennsylvania, Val worked summers, driving a taxi in New York.

When I met Val, I loved him. He had a great love for people and a wonderful sense of humor. However, he had zero interest in visiting Romania. Many people were jealous of those who escaped, and he was afraid of how he would be treated, even though he now has an American passport. He was especially afraid of the secret police, many of whom were still around. I prevailed, and Val had a change of heart for which I am grateful. Val's English was pretty good, and I asked him, "How did you learn to speak English?"

"Well," he replied, "every night, I would watch the *Honeymooners*." He had many Ralph and Norton-like expressions! He knew every single line of some of the episodes. He would entertain me for hours on the flights over and back with Val *Honeymooner* reruns! Val made many trips with me over the years, and we became great friends.

C H A P T E R   1 0

Desperate for Medicine

The first trip with Val, we were introduced to the director of the children's hospital in Bucharest, Dr. Stratt. I was shocked to learn that they had so little medical supplies for the children. I visited a hospital where the surgeons were operating without even masks over their faces. They had wrapped towels around them, trying to be sterile. They had so many needs, but their greatest need was for antibiotics. I returned home and contacted some friends that worked at the corporate office of Rite Aid drugstores. They were wonderful and promised to donate thousands of dollars of antibiotics as well as other medication for the children of Romania if I could get a local doctor to be involved.

Dr. Howard Miller, a wonderful doctor in my community, was happy to help. I made an impassioned call to Delta Airlines. After a lengthy conversation, with the right person, they promised to ship in the cargo of the airplane as much medication as we could bring to JFK, then fly it to Budapest, where, then, we would deliver by a rental van to Romania. I had made a reservation for a van in Budapest and was feeling pretty confident that all would go smoothly.

I had a van full of medication and supplies. We had packed them in two-by-two-foot boxes, four feet high. I brought at least sixteen with me to Kennedy airport, a seven-hour trip. Stopping in Williamsport, Pennsylvania, I picked up Val and continued on. We unloaded at Kennedy, and Delta received them into cargo. The overnight flight was uneventful, and we landed in Budapest in the morning.

We went through customs, no problem, and then waited at the designated area for the boxes of medication. In about forty-five minutes, they appeared. I pulled out all the information for the van rental and walked to the counter, confident that all would be well. Giving my information to the agent, he began searching the computer for my reservation. In very broken English, he looked at me and said these crazy words. "Sorry, sir, but we have no van for you."

"No, that's impossible," I replied. "Please check again."

To no avail, he did and then explained something to me that really set me back. "We do not have your reservation, and I have checked with all that lease here. There is no van available." He went on to explain that only so many vans are leased that go to Romania. "It is because of theft," he explained, "and all vans that can legally be leased for Romania are already leased. You will not find a van."

Now, for the very religious, you may want to skip this part. I was very upset at God, and I told him so. How can we come this far, and then He can't even make sure we have a van? "Really? I'm doing my part." It went very downhill from there. After about an hour of total unconsciousness and very angry words, I began to calm. To be perfectly honest, I did not act very spiritual and said some very negative things to God about what a lousy job He was doing. I would rather not repeat them. We also had a serious conversation about choosing me. There were so many things that needed to be done. How will I accomplish them? There are so many more qualified, why me?

I remember Gideon's reaction (in the Old Testament) when he was asked to do something he knew he was incapable of doing. "Of all of the people you could ask, I am the least," was his reply. I was angry at God and the inadequacy in myself. A bad combination. It's written that when we ask, it is with hands open without wrath or doubt in our hearts. I unclenched my fists toward God and opened my hands to Him, knowing the only way out of this mess is through Him. "Sorry about those mean things I said, I could use a little help. Certainly, we have not come this far to fail." I sat down and breathed.

There was a man I had noticed near the rental office, where I had received the news of no van. Please remember, this is Budapest, Hungary. Very few, if any, spoke English. Their first language was

Hungarian, and their second was Russian. Suddenly, out of the crowd, he approached me and, in perfect English, asked, "Do you need a van?"

"Do I need a van!" I answered in perfect English. "Yes!" I am in shock and disbelief. Oh yes, this is a God thing.

He walked me outside, and there was a red Fiat van. Just the right size. "How much?" I said, still staggering.

"Whatever is fair," he replied.

I pressed $600 into his hands, which is what the van was supposed to cost. He handed me the keys, agreed to the time of my return, and disappeared into the crowd. I remembered, wondering, do we need any papers to cross the border with this van? We quickly ran to find the man, but it was too late; he was gone.

Stolen Van at the Border?

The drive to the border is about three hours, and I knew of two different entry points that I had used previously where you could enter Romania. By the map, I chose the shortest route and was on my way. My mind began to think of my situation, and the thoughts went crazy. Val and I began to wonder, is this a stolen van? Are there any papers legally allowing this van to leave the country? We searched the glove box and found nothing that looked anything like insurance papers or even registration. So here we are with a stolen van, loaded with prescription medicine. What could possibly go wrong?

By the time we got to the border, we were in such fear, and I was sure "Stolen Van" was written on my forehead in Hungarian! Pulling up to the guards, the very first question they asked was, "Where are the papers for the van?" Reaching into the glove box, the only thing we found looked like a receipt from McDonald's, really. "You cannot leave the country," the soldier declared. "You do not have the correct papers." He ordered us to return to get the papers we needed.

I turned the car around and pulled off the road. Who is failing here? Me or God? "Okay," I said. "You gave me the medicine, you put into the heart of Delta to fly it for free, and then some man gives me a van, a total stranger, but you forgot a few small details, like the papers we need to drive this thing!" Remember lifting hands without wrath or doubt? I wasn't doing that. It is amazing when we move from faith to doubt, how it usually leads to anger toward God. All we have to do is believe, remove the sign from our foreheads "Stolen

Van," change it to "Miracle Van," and change our conversation. How great it was going to be when we reached Lipova.

We headed south to the next crossing. I could see, in my mind, us crossing over without any trouble. And we began to talk about how easy it was going to be. A few hours later, without any interest at all in the van, our passports were stamped, and we were on the way to deliver life-saving medicine to the helpless.

One humorous story during that trip was when the muffler came loose, and we had to get it fixed. I did not want to return the van to this kind man, broken. We pulled into an auto shop in the middle of the country. "Can you fix the car?" Val asked.

"Yes," he said, "right after our break." Well, a Romanian break ended up being a soccer game for over an hour behind the shop. We were in no hurry and were most entertained. We enjoyed talking to the owner as we waited and were just thankful for an auto shop. We returned the van to the airport, could not find the gentleman, so we left it where we picked it up and flew back to America. God gets involved when you do good to those who cannot do good in return and does for you what you cannot do for yourself.

C H A P T E R   1 2

In the Dark of Night

*H*aving Val with me was wonderful, but we noticed the animosity that many of the guards at the Romanian border had toward him. They would see an American passport, but when he spoke, and they saw his Romanian name, they realized he was a Romanian, and they would treat him with disrespect. I was grateful communism was gone, but the mentality of the people was the same, and many from the old regime were still in power. I remember one such event as we were returning to Budapest to catch our flight back to JFK and then the drive to Pennsylvania.

It was about 2:00 a.m., as our flight was leaving early from Budapest. We had only so much time to get through the border and to the airport. The line of cars leaving Romania was at least two miles long. The road was very narrow, and I did not want to drive up the wrong side, so we got out of the car and walked to the front of the line. It was so dark and scary. There was a real battle between my fear and my faith. I was petrified. Guards stopped us, and I began to explain our situation. Val would always try to remain silent because of the mistreatment he would receive.

Grabbing both of our passports, he asked Val, "Where are you from? You are not an American." Screaming in anger, knowing that Val had escaped from Romania, he came unglued. Another guard quickly appeared with a German shepherd. The dog began to snarl and bark. That was enough for me. We turned around and headed back to the car. I remember it was just before Thanksgiving, and I wanted to be home. I wanted to be safe, and I wanted out of this place. We waited for about an hour, and then I said, "Val, we must go."

I started the car and began driving toward the front of the line on the wrong side of the road. Thankfully, we did not encounter traffic coming the other way, and soon we could see the border guards. I drove directly to the front of the line. The same guard who had previously screamed and went ballistic on us came up to the window. It was as if he was blind to me jumping the line, and he was polite. He acted like he had never seen me before. "Passports, please," he said politely. He walked into the guardhouse, stamped our passports, and we crossed into Hungary. When you do good to those who can never do you good in return, God does for you what you cannot do for yourself! It was my best Thanksgiving ever.

CHAPTER 13

Kidnapped?

It was the early '90s, and the war in Yugoslavia, now called Serbia and Montenegro, was raging. During this time, we made many trips, bringing medical supplies, musical instruments, and things for our growing orphanage. Many people were fleeing the country, and there was chaos. We were not aware of the problems we would encounter. We had another van full of medicine and supplies, landed in Budapest, rented a van, and headed to the Romanian border. On this trip, I was accompanied by Pastor Jim Finn. Five miles before we reached the border, we were shocked to see the line. Usually, there are a few cars, and it would be no big deal. This time, we had a huge problem.

Most of these people in line were fleeing the war. The Hungarians did not want them, and the Romanians did not want them. So the line was literally five miles long, just waiting for something to happen. Some spoke broken English and had been waiting for days! This would not work. So we decided to jump the line, drive up the wrong side of the road, and try to reach the front of the line as we had done previously. All went well for about a mile, but suddenly, we were stopped by two policemen on motorcycles. "Back of the line," they ordered us, and we obeyed. Delivering us to the back of the line, the police continued back in the direction of Budapest, so we decided to try again! This time, we only got about three miles before we were stopped.

In Hungarian, there was a big discussion about us to someone on the police radio. We were turned around and escorted to the back of the line again. This time, instead of leaving us there, we were ordered to follow the police away from the border and back toward Budapest. I was afraid and thought we were going to be arrested. Suddenly, the police pulled off the main road to a dirt road and headed deep into the country. In about fifteen minutes, we reached an army blockade on the road. The police had a quick conversation with the army, and they opened up the road and motioned us to follow. This is where I pretty much lost faith. We were not being arrested, we were being kidnapped in the middle of God knows where, and they will steal our supplies, sell them, and kill us. Great thoughts of faith!

We decided to hit the brakes, turn around, go the other way, and then pray. At that instant, before we acted, we found ourselves at the front of the line. We were not being kidnapped; we had been detoured around all that traffic and then hand-delivered to the customs official. Our passports were stamped, and we were in Romania. We were afraid, but God is a great partner! When we do good to those who can do us no good in return, God will do for you what you cannot do for yourself.

C H A P T E R   1 4

Do It Afraid

I have shared a few stories, in the previous chapters, of times I was in great fear. Another time was on a cold winter night in the mid-1990s, and I had booked another trip with Jim Finn to fly Delta Airlines out of JFK. We were a couple of hours out over the Atlantic Ocean, chatting about what we planned to accomplish. It was getting close to dinnertime, and we were preparing to eat. Suddenly, the captain, on the loudspeaker, ordered everyone to return to their seats at once and put on their seat belts. There was no turbulence, but we suddenly smelled smoke. Turning around, to our horror, we saw the whole back of the plane was full of smoke. The flight attendants were running to the back of the plane with fire extinguishers, and people started screaming. I looked at Jim and said, "We're going to die." By the look on his face, he agreed. As you can see, we didn't die. In fact, the fire was put out, and we had dinner shortly afterward.

No matter how great your vision is, you will face these moments of fear. Perhaps the greater your vision or purpose, the greater the fear will be. In the back part of our brain, where our head meets our neck, is our fear center. This part of the brain is about one thing, survival. When we face a threat, all of our thinking moves to this part of our brain. On the front part of our brain is where we think rationally, where we know love, where our dreams and hopes live. This is also the place of our faith. As you can see, faith and fear live just inches apart! So you must learn how they can live together.

There was a woman by the name of Elisabeth Elliot who was born into a missionary family in Brussels. Before she was a year old, they moved to America and settled in Germantown, Pennsylvania. Elisabeth grew up and attended Wheaton College. There she met Jim Elliot. After graduation, Elisabeth went on a missionary expedition to Ecuador with other students from Wheaton, including Jim Elliot. They were married in 1953 and continued to serve in Ecuador.

Elisabeth's husband and his missionary partner were brutally murdered by the same people they were trying to help. After that tragedy, her life was completely controlled by fear. She felt, in her heart, she was to continue the work her husband started but was paralyzed by that fear. One day, she was telling her friend of her vision to continue her husband's work but also how full of fear she was. Her friend replied, "Why don't you just do it afraid?"

Being stuck in fear, worried about possible outcomes, and afraid to take the first step keeps us from the place where faith grows. So why not just do it afraid? Even if your knees are shaking, *step out*. Even if you feel you're not enough, *step out*. Even if you feel many could do it better, *step out*. Elisabeth stepped out, went on to work with the Indian tribes of Ecuador, including the very people who had killed her husband. Elisabeth wrote many books, inspired thousands of people, and did it afraid. So to answer the question, yes, I was often afraid. When you do it afraid, your faith is activated by taking the step. Reverend Martin Luther King Jr. said, "Faith is taking the first step even when you don't see the whole staircase."

CHAPTER 15

Outdated Medicine

*M*any trips were made bringing medicine to Romania, some by vans to Budapest, and some with me directly by airplane to Bucharest. One such flight I will never forget. It was the winter season, and I had booked a flight from Buffalo to JFK, and then to Bucharest. I was able to put four boxes of medicine and antibiotics in the car to take with me to the children. Two of the four boxes were outdated just a little but still good, and two of the boxes were not outdated and good for a long time. They were in unmarked boxes, two-by-two feet and four feet high. When I arrived at the airport, we had just finished a snowstorm, many flights had been canceled, and the plane was full. The flight attendant apologized to me and explained that because the flight was so full, I could only bring two boxes. This really confused and upset me, but I obliged.

On the trip to New York and all the way to Bucharest, I complained to God. "You could at least control the weather."

In the morning, I arrived in Bucharest and was greeted by Dr. Stratt from the children's hospital. "Do you have any outdated medicine?" he asked.

"Why?" I answered.

"Yesterday, a law was passed that if anyone brought outdated medicine to Romania, they could be arrested. A child had died, and the Romanians had blamed the death on outdated donated medicine given from another country," he continued.

Great, I thought, *do I have the two boxes with outdated medicine or the others?* Remember, when you're doing good for those who cannot do you good in return? Yes, that's right, when they opened the boxes, they were both the up-to-date medicine and antibiotics. What an adventure!

One humorous story I would like to share is about Rod Stewart. On one of my trips to Romania, I noticed quite a fanfare in first class. I was told it was Rod Stewart flying to Bucharest for a concert. When we arrived in Bucharest, there was a party of people with flowers waiting at the bottom of the plane. *For Rod Stewart*, I thought, *a very important person*. As I disembarked, I noticed Rod Stewart standing with one other person, and the welcome committee paid him no mind. The welcome party was for me! It was a group of doctors and nurses from the children's hospital, complete with a bouquet of flowers. I was dying to know what Rod Stewart thought as he stood by himself, and I was the dignitary! Tonight was not his night!

CHAPTER 16

No Bribe, No Approval

I noticed many times during my trips to Romania, in the early '90s, people were flying home with a baby adopted from Romania. I remember a conversation with a mother who had adopted a baby. The cost for her to adopt was $30,000! *This cannot be right*, I thought. And my second thought was, *What about the older children?* Everyone wanted a baby, but there were many older children. Under the communist dictator, who was propped up by the Soviet Union, birth control was outlawed in the country. Children were, by the hundreds, simply left at the doors of state-run orphanages because the families could not afford to feed them. I visited many of these orphanages, and it broke my heart.

Under communist rule, the secret police were everywhere. In proportion to the population of America, ten million of the people living in the country would be spies for the government. Trials were a joke, and swift punishment would come to anyone who even spoke against the regime. Bribery and corruption were considered normal, and even after the fall of communism, much of the corruption continued.

Through the contacts I had made with the children's clinics, I was able to meet with an attorney who helped with adoptions in Romania. We met in the lobby of a hotel in Bucharest. She was very pleasant, but the bottom line, $50,000 had to be paid first. It was not called a bribe, it was called a donation, but it was a bribe for sure. I was not going to pay this money as I knew it was wrong.

Back in America, I began the process of starting an international adoption agency. I needed two very important pieces of this puzzle. First, apply for the license. Then I had to have a director and a social worker on staff. We went through the process in Pennsylvania, hired a director, Andy Lehman, a wonderful man, as well as Helene Elco, our social worker. With all completed, I returned to Romania. Ten times I was promised our accreditation, but every trip to Bucharest ended up with them wanting money. Some changes were made in the government, and a new ministry of health was appointed. I had visited that office many times with the previous minister to no avail. I felt I had a better chance with the new minister.

I booked the trip and, without an appointment, was able to have a meeting with the new minister of health. Since I had been there many times with the old minister, I knew exactly where the office was. He was a very nice gentleman but explained to me that they have thousands of applications for approval of adoption agencies from all around the world. It would be impossible for him to find our application. I prevailed upon him to let me look where they were kept and see if I could find it. "Just give me five minutes to look," I pleaded.

He was so good about it and led me to a room that was about ten-by-ten feet. Opening the door, I saw, not in a neat order, but just thrown on the floor, a huge pile of applications from all over the world. Hundreds of them all in a pile on the floor. He left me alone and returned to his office.

In frustration, I simply kicked into the pile. Not a very spiritual thing to do, but when the bunch I kicked landed back on the pile, there, in front of me, was my application! Even if you're frustrated, God is still with you. Picking it up, I walked into his office, and he approved New Life International for adoptions. No bribe paid. When you do for others who can never do you good in return, God does for you what you cannot do for yourself! Later, I will share the stories of a few of these beautiful children that came to live in America (in chapters 24, 25, 26).

CHAPTER 17

Depressed and Bald

In July of 1996, I was returning from Romania on TWA, a Boeing 747-100. I had flown from Romania to Rome, then back to America on TWA. The plane was very old, but I was not worried as it had been used since the early '70s, and I trusted the older planes. We were about halfway home, and they were serving lunch. I was seated by the window with a sweet elderly couple in the two seats beside me. We put down our trays, and our food was served. Suddenly, for the first and only time in my life, I had a panic attack. I could not stay in that seat one more second. "Please, let me out," I pleaded.

The poor old couple had to lift their trays, hand them to the flight attendant, pull themselves out of their seats so that I could get out. I ran to the restroom, locked the door behind me, and looked in the mirror. For real, I did not recognize myself. It was really weird. I remember walking up and down the aisles of that plane, thinking, *What in the world is wrong with me?*

I made it home okay, but I had this feeling of total apathy. Not only apathy but total loss of appetite. I could not sleep, even for five minutes. All I could see was that something was wrong. The last straw was the loss of my hair. Every morning, in the shower, I would see my hair falling out by the gobs. I went to my local doctor who sent me to another doctor, and after many tests, they determined that I had clinical depression. So they gave me Ambien, Zoloft, and Ativan.

Depression was one thing, but I could not do depression and bald together. I am sure bald is beautiful, but I wasn't quite ready to embrace that thinking at forty years old. So I headed to Buffalo, New

York, and found a place where they instantly restore your hair. Some call it a wig; they called it the unit. I liked their terminology better. Feeling so much better about myself, I returned home, walked into the house, and was told that it looked like a dead animal was on my head. LOL. I am sure they were correct.

The combination of the three medications made my condition worse. The absolute terrifying thing would be the nightmares. I would fall asleep on the couch, and then in my dream, a man would come out of the fireplace with a large knife. We would wrestle forever, it seemed. I knew it was a dream but could not wake up. It was horrifying.

During this period, I was asked to speak at a church in Greensburg, Pennsylvania. This was a very large church called the Word of Life with Pastor Tom Walters. It was a Saturday evening, and I was a few miles from the hotel I would be staying at. I was approaching the red light and having a conversation in my head about whether it is a red light or a green light.

Suddenly, I was right behind the car in front of me, stopped as the light was red. At fifty miles per hour, I slammed into the back of that car so hard that the seats broke, and the occupants were both literally lying down in the car. When I slammed into the car, the unit escaped my head. It was held on by a couple of clips, but they were not built for impact. LOL. The airbag exploded on my steering wheel, and the unit spun around and landed pinned to my face. The car was full of smoke, and this hairy thing was on my face. I thought I had died and this was hell. I realized what had happened and tried to secure the unit back onto my head. I did not realize, until later, when I looked into the mirror, that it was actually sideways on my head.

A state trooper was very close by, and within minutes, he was at my window. I rolled it down. He looked at me with my unit on sideways and said, "Sir, are you okay? Have you been drinking?"

To which I answered, "No, but I have depression."

The state trooper said, "Well, it looks like no one is hurt, but I think you totaled both cars."

The tow truck driver took my car to an auto body shop and helped me secure a rental. Getting to my hotel, I somehow slept a few hours without a nightmare and made it to the meeting in the morning. I never knew the cause of that panic attack, but I do know that shortly after, by a few days, one of the same model planes that I flew in, the Boeing 747-100, on the same flight that I took over, Flight 800, crashed and killed many people. You may remember that terrible event. I always wondered if somehow, in my spirit, I felt what would happen. I returned home and said, "I cannot live this way any longer."

There were a few ladies that would pray in our church every Wednesday morning. They knew of my situation; it was pretty obvious. A unit on my head, I never smiled, and I had lost twenty-five pounds. They asked if they could pray for me. "Sure," I said, "the doctors haven't helped me. Let's try this."

Now these ladies prayed unlike any other I had ever witnessed. One said nothing, one shook me, one said, "Hold on," one said, "Let go," one stood at the back of the church and cursed out depression, literally using words I had never heard in a church before! And one was not even praying in English.

Now I had suffered for months, and I was not going to judge. After about an hour, I stood up, and I knew it was over. I threw all my medications away that day and slept like a baby that night. Why? I have a destiny, and in spite of me, I will fulfill it. You cannot mess up your destiny. You're not that good or bad enough.

He Said No Way

The transformation from pig farm to an orphanage was done with money from our church, local businesses in Pennsylvania along with labor from Romanian workers. To build the orphanage, the methods and building materials were so poor we decided we would ship containers across the ocean and take our own team to build the church. I am not a carpenter, and I needed one desperately. At that time, our town was growing because of a local corporation, Adelphia. The contractors were all very busy building high-end homes for the executives of the corporation. Jim Neefe, a childhood friend, was a contractor and member of our church. He met his wife, Julie, at this church as well. They had been married for quite a long time and wanted but could not have children. "I need you, Jim," I begged.

His reply, "Impossible!"

All the men coming with me had taken their vacations and paid for their own tickets. Not one was being paid. It was a pure gift of love.

Jim and his wife had tried everything to have a child and spent much money to no avail. Many doctors had worked with them, but no child. I prevailed upon him often as we were preparing for the trip, but he always said no. I could not even get his wife to convince him. As we were getting the container loaded for the trip to Baltimore and then across the water, Jim had a change of heart. "I really am too busy, but I feel I cannot say no," he said.

Two days before we were leaving for Romania, the child welfare director called Jim and Julie. I have a brand-new healthy baby boy for you! Within a few hours, Marshal Neefe was in the arms of his mother. I want you, the reader, to comprehend one powerful truth. When you do good to someone who can never do good in return, God will do for you what you cannot do for yourself. It is called the realm of miracles for you and the one you have helped.

It wasn't until a few years later we found out about how exactly Jim and Julie got this child. Two years after the trip, I was visiting a local bank and talking to the banker. He shared with me a story of how they had been waiting for a child. The day the call came that a baby boy was available, both his wife and he prayed and felt God told them that this was not their child, even though the baby was actually born on the banker's birthday. They told the social worker to allow another couple to adopt this baby. Guess who was next on the list? The baby was delivered to the door of Jim and Julie Neefe. They didn't even know the full story until years later when I shared with them the banker's story.

Everything we needed to build the first phase of the building was on the container—plywood, trusses, windows, roofing, generator, exterior concrete board, and lumber. The weight was crazy, over sixty tons. Anyone who understands trucking knows that this amount is overweight for the highways. We did not mean to do so, but we needed everything in the container. So we had to ship it overweight.

We had a professional driver, James Johns, a member of our church, all scheduled to drive to the port in Baltimore. I convinced him to take the overweight trailer to the port. We had no choice. We had to get the material to Romania. We prayed our best prayer, and he was on his way. Two tire blowouts on the way to the port, and eighteen hours later, the container was on the ship. Soon, we would join it in Lipova.

Jim had calculated that if we have seven days to work and worked twelve hours a day, we could build the total exterior. This would mean the walls, trusses, siding, windows, and all the interior framing. We had twelve volunteers, some who knew a little, and some who were office workers. The day flight to Romania was uneventful. We arrived exhausted but eager to build.

CHAPTER 19

We Have Seventy-Two Hours

*H*ouston, we have a problem. Our container was being held up in customs, and there was a great concern. This problem is usually over a bribe of which I hated the thought of. Held up one day, then two days, then three days. We were running out of time. Men had paid their own way. They had taken their vacations. I looked incompetent, and it looked like we would not build. In desperation, I called a friend in America who was an aid to the Senator Rick Santorum. I'm not sure how he did it, but our container was released and on the way. We were very appreciative to the senator for his assistance.

There are a couple of ways into the city of Lipova where we were going to build. The driver took the shortest route without realizing that the bridge going into the city was very old, like over a hundred years, and it was rated for less than seven tons. It should have been condemned years ago. The truck arrived at three in the morning but had stopped at the bridge. The driver is refusing to cross the bridge and to get to a bridge that could be safe would lose an extra day. We prayed, and because we were desperate, we had no other choice than to believe.

With great persuasion and the promise of money, we convinced the driver to cross the bridge. It was like the crossing of the Red Sea. The noises that old bridge made were unbelievable, but we came over on dry ground. The driver refused to take the bridge after the container was empty and took the long way home. He said he knew God was with him the first time but didn't want to chance it again!

The Romanians were so excited to have the container finally on the property, thinking they were doing us a favor, unloaded it into a great big pile. All had been sorted in America in such a way that we could assemble it easily. But each item needed to be unloaded in a particular order. It took four hours to sort it all out, and we started the generator and began to build!

The building of that church would make a book in itself. The language barrier alone made it quite challenging. So many stories of every man who worked so diligently hour after hour. After a short nap when exhaustion hit, they were right back to work. In the evening, the generator literally glowed in the dark because it was so hot. Even though it was brand-new, they are not meant to run continuously, but ours did. A few times it died but was resurrected by some prayer and interesting backyard engineering. I do want to share one event that halted our project dead in its tracks, kind of like how the bridge stopped us.

We had trusses premade for the exact size of the blueprints. The only problem is that the Romanians had made the foundation two feet over what the plans called for. That meant the trusses we had shipped would be two feet short. Anyone who understands building can comprehend exactly what we were up against. "We're done," Jim declared.

"We are not done," was my answer.

"You don't understand," Jim said. "These are engineered to sit exactly on top of the wall. They are too short and cannot work. We need a new set of trusses. It is the only way."

"Jimmy, listen to me. Go someplace quiet and ask God, the Master Builder, to help you," I responded.

With clipboard in hand, shaking his head, Jimmy headed into a distant field. Everyone else just looked at each other in disbelief. How could we have come this far, our container arrived, and we witnessed the miracle of the bridge? And now what?

About an hour later, Jim is back! "Okay," he declared, "start ripping the trusses apart!" Jim explained his plan to me. Now this was sounding either crazy or all God. These were intricate small and large pieces all fitted together. They were locked together with steel brackets that had to all be torn off. We then had to recut all the intricate pieces to fit the new truss we were making. It literally looked like a total disaster area. It took all the men, both Romanians and Americans, about five hours, but we totally dismantled those factory-built, pre-engineered, perfect and very expensive trusses. Then we rebuilt them all to the new God specifications.

One by one, they were built and raised to the top of the wall! I did not understand the miracle until later in conversation with the truss engineer. He said it was *impossible* that any contractor could have had the knowledge to do what was done in Romania. He had no idea how it could have physically been done.

Seventy-two hours from start to finish, the men were done. A celebration was held in the new church. Although tired, the feeling of accomplishment and the knowing they had made a difference for eternity, these men's lives were changed in so many ways. They witnessed how God gets involved when we help those who can do us no good in return. We would return in the future to finish the inside of the building.

As a sidenote, a few years later, a terrible storm passed through the city, and many people from the factory across the road from the church sought refuge in the church, a building where God was the engineer.

C H A P T E R   2 0

Two Times, Two Boys

Jim Neefe went with me two times to Romania. The second time was to finish the inside of the building. This time, I asked, and without hesitation, he said yes. He would not miss it for the world. Jim reminded me, "Last time, God gave me a son. How can I say no!"

A second container was loaded to be shipped to Romania. We put the whole interior along with a dental clinic on the second container. It had been donated to me from a local teaching college. On the container were drywall, wiring, ceiling system, paint, fixtures, right down to the carpet, and tile. A team was brought together, and we made the trip again to Lipova, Romania. This trip was very smooth. With only a few minor problems, we were able to finish the inside, and Sunday morning had the first service in the new building. The building was almost full, and the people were so happy.

Guess what happened? My brother, Judge Stephen Minor, who was a local attorney at that time, was contacted by a family looking for help in finding a home for their teenage daughter's baby soon to come. They wanted a good loving family. Steve and Jim grew up together and remained friends throughout the years. Guess who Steve called? You guessed it, Jim and Julie. Are you getting the message? What doctors and medical science could not do for Jim and Julie, God did two times, every time Jim helped those who could never do him good in return. I asked Jim if he wanted to go a third time. "No," he said. "Two boys are enough!"

C H A P T E R   2 1

Don't Leave Me Now!

One of the pastors had found a large tent for sale. It could seat approximately 1,400 people, and it included the tractor, trailer, stage, and chairs. We raised the money and made the purchase. Hunedoara, a few hours north of Lipova, was a place of great poverty, with many sick people as well as a criminal element. Here, we wanted to put up this huge tent and invite people to come and hear a positive message. Under communism, there was never hope, and the mentality was very difficult to change. To change a mind, you must first touch the heart. It was not going to be just words but actions that touched the people. We would offer them hope, not a dead God but a living hope. That is what we planned to do.

It had been a while since Pastor Jim Finn had been with me to Romania. I asked him if he would come with me to Hunedoara for this great outdoor event. I told him we would have music, and we would market it well so many would come, and he agreed. Now Pastor Finn had seen many miracles. He had special faith to pray for the sick, and I thought that would be a great way to advertise.

Communism had taught the people that God is dead. Churches were either shut down or the few that were allowed to be open, many of the pastors were actually members of the secret police and would report the people for being there. God was indeed dead to this country. So I decided to make hundreds of signs that we put all over the city. They said, "Come and see the miracles of a living God. The lame will walk, the blind will see, and the deaf will hear." I was confident, with the faith of Jim Finn, we would have a great time.

53

An interesting sidenote I found out later was how the tent was erected. The tent was to be erected a few days before we were to arrive. The problem was, not one of the Romanians had any idea how to raise it. It was huge, literally a circus tent. Down the center were long poles, at least thirty feet in the air. It was something that required knowledge as putting it up wrong could cause injury and even death. This story was told to me after I arrived.

The men arrived at the soccer field where the tent was to be erected, unloaded everything, and then looked at each other. A few minutes later, a young man, about sixteen or seventeen years old, appeared on a bicycle. "Do you need some help?" he asked. "I help every year when the circus comes to town. I know exactly what to do." And he did. Within six hours, the tent was erected. All were so excited to see what would happen under that tent.

I believe it was a Wednesday, and Pastor Finn had agreed to meet me at JFK. I flew from Buffalo, New York, and waited for him to arrive. It was getting later and later, and soon, we had to board the flight. I had tried to call Jim but no answer. When I could get through to him, he explained he had an emergency and could not make the trip! Are you kidding me? Signs all over the city in Hunedoara, 1,400-seat tent erected, I told them 400 seats were more than enough, sick people are coming to be healed, and all they get is me! Very few that I ever prayed for in the past, that I can remember, got healed. Really, my track record was pitiful. I was not a man of faith. It was a long flight, with a lot of God conversation. Most of it was about how embarrassed I was going to be when I had to explain that the great miracle man missed the plane.

It was the very first night, the night they would see great miracles. The pastors in Romania did not seem too upset, but I was. If they were expecting me to be the miracle worker, they were sadly misguided. I called my dear father back in America and explained my situation. "What in the world should I do?" I asked him.

"You don't have to do anything. They don't know the great man of faith isn't there, so just tell them about faith and what God can and will do," he answered.

We had some wonderful musicians, and they played and sang. It was much enjoyed, but then came the moment of truth. I will never forget how inadequate I felt. I thought of the many great speakers and men of faith who could do a much better job than me. As the title of this book says, not because of me but in spite of me. With no other choice, I began to tell of how faith moves mountains and that God honors faith in any nation or people and how He wanted to heal their land and bodies. I may have spoken for fifteen minutes and then asked if there were any sick. Well, my friend, there were many. I will tell you of a few who God touched that night.

One deaf man began to hear, all to my surprise. Another, who said he was blind in one eye, began to see again out of that eye. One lady, who was stooped over, stood straight up and began to dance. Honestly, one by one, as they were getting healed, I thought they were faking their healing just like I was faking my great faith because I had none! This went on until there was one man left. He was a crippled man, his knees were bowed together, and two men helped him walk to where I was, at the front of the tent. Suddenly, I knew I was in trouble. This man is surely crippled, and everyone knows it. I closed my eyes and could not even whisper a word. As we stood there in silence, suddenly an ear-piercing scream shook me, and I opened my eyes to see him running around that tent. People were clapping and cheering. I was in shock.

One lady came running up next to me, all dressed in black. "Who is this lady?" I asked my interpreter, who was also dancing for joy.

"She is a gypsy and a witch."

"What is she saying?" I asked. The people were still shouting as the man was still running.

"She is telling you that she has never believed before, but now she wants this new life. She had been his neighbor for sixteen years and had never seen him even take a step."

The whole miracle was on video from start to finish, and I remember watching it that night. The Romanians wanted to put it on YouTube, but the next day, somehow, it disappeared. That's okay. It was never about me. It was the faith of the people who never got the message that the man of faith could not make it. When you do good for those who can never do you good in return, God does for you what you cannot do for yourself.

C H A P T E R   2 2

Breaking Ponies in Montana

Still in shock and disbelief, I returned home to America. Bill and Barb Halderman were members of our church in Pennsylvania. Bill was a professional fly fisherman who owned a beautiful lodge and restaurant near our town. Surrounding this lodge were many small lakes that he had stocked with many different kinds of trout. He would have people come from all over to learn his fly-fishing method and stay at his lodge. He appeared very successful. Bill was being treated by a chiropractor, who was also a member of our church. Bill began to open up to the doctor that he was having marital problems and was unsure where to look for help. "My pastor would be happy to talk to you," Dr. Fink explained to Bill. "You don't need to be a member of the church." The doctor called me, and of course, I was happy to meet with Bill.

Bill made an appointment, and we met a few days later. Bill talked about his marriage and his business. They were under a lot of stress with the business as well as personal problems. "Bill," I said, "what would it look like to your wife if you went home and said to her, 'Honey, I want to be a better man for you'?"

"Perhaps, if I go to church, it would help me to become that man," he answered.

"Then invite her to come with you, and let's see what happens," I replied.

We prayed a short prayer together, and Bill headed home.

Sunday morning, both Bill and Barb were in church and absolutely loved the service. Soon, they were members, and we were blessed to have them.

Around a year after Bill and Barb joined our church, he called me from the local hospital. "Can you come and see me?" he said. And, of course, I was on my way to him. Bill told me how the doctors had run some tests, and they did not like what they saw. Bill had been in Vietnam and was exposed to Agent Orange. This was our greatest fear.

Bill was taken to Pittsburgh, where they would operate on him. When they opened him up, they discovered the cancer was so widespread that they could do nothing but close him up and, when he came to, they gave him two choices. "Your first choice, we can treat with chemo and radiation but you have a 2 percent chance of surviving. The second choice is to do nothing and die," the doctor explained.

Bill replied, "Well, 2 percent is better than zero, so let's do it."

A few months into his treatment, Bill got the bad news that it did not work, and he had, maybe, a month to live. When the news came to me, I got in my car and headed for Pittsburgh. That was a long and very thoughtful trip.

What do you say to a dying man? What do you say to his wife and his children? I had been in this place way too many times. Finding Bill's room at the hospital was quite a challenge, but I found him and how pitiful he looked. He was a shell of a man. He had lost so much weight, he was completely bald from head to foot, and he looked like a refugee in a concentration camp. I knew I would be preaching his funeral in just a few days. When he would speak, I was barely able to hear him. His throat was so burnt from the radiation. "I have a dream," he said to me.

"Good, Bill, what is it?" I asked.

"I want to move to Montana and buy a ranch and break ponies like I did when I was young."

His dear wife rolled her eyes and looked at me.

"How are you going to do that, Bill?" I asked.

"Well," he said, "I have a life insurance policy for one hundred thousand dollars. I can sell it today for eighty thousand dollars to a company that buys these from people who are supposed to die soon." Then he said, "I will sell the lodge, and with the money from both the lodge and the insurance policy, I will buy a ranch in Montana."

I hoped the look on my face wasn't too crazy, but this talk was. So I said, "Well, what about the reports?"

Three review boards had said he was going to die. One of these boards had been hired by the company buying his life insurance policy. Wow, and now he expects me to do something? With my words, I said all the right things in my prayer that day with Bill, but in my mind, I knew for sure that I would be getting a call soon that he had passed.

Now, over twenty years later, Bill lives on! He went to Montana, bought a ranch, broke ponies, and moved to Fort Myers, Florida, to fish again! I remember a conversation I had with Bill a few years ago. "How did you get healed, Bill? I know it was not my faith. I thought for sure you were going to die." It reminded me of the miracle I saw under the tent in Hunedoara, where, in spite of what I believed, the power was in their faith, not mine.

In his mind, I was some great man of faith, so he was prepared to live. One thing Bill told me that was so important is that every thought that came to him saying he would die, he would give it to God and replace it with the thought of breaking ponies in Montana. He would not allow anyone to come into his room without a smile. And he never thought of dying again.

Our dominant thought will always determine our level of faith. It was not my prayer or my faith. It was simply his. You can only soar as high as your highest thoughts. Bill's highest thoughts were about living, and today, twenty-four years later, he is the only man I ever heard of who collected his life insurance and lived on!

CHAPTER 23

Too Busy Praying

Some people make a mark on your life. One of these people for me was Ellie Armstrong. Many years ago, Ellie was written up in the *Guidepost* magazine, a very popular publication at that time. I believe it is still published today.

Ellie was a school teacher in New York State and had come down with a very serious disease. In short, Ellie was dying, but God intervened, and Ellie was healed. Ellie was so excited about what had happened to her that she quit her job, convinced her sister, Roberta, also to quit her job as a teacher, moved to Pennsylvania, and bought a motel. Every room in the motel had a different name. If you had depression, they had a room; cancer, a room; diabetes, a room. I think you get the picture. People came from all over to stay at Ellie's Motel. Many were healed, and her story is written for all to read.

Just one of the many that I remember was a lady with arthritis. Her husband had driven her to Ellie's as she could not even open the car door because her hands were all disfigured. Ellie put her in the arthritis room and went to bed. In the middle of the night, she was awakened to the sound of a car door opening and slamming shut, again and again. Ellie went out into the parking lot, and the lady with the arthritis was there. "Ellie," she said, "look, I am healed. I can open the door again." Her hands were totally made whole.

One morning, Ellie had this overwhelming feeling that God was going to visit her today. How often does this happen? She had never felt this before and told her sister, "Roberta, I don't care if the president of the United States shows up. Do not disturb me for any reason. I believe something amazing is going to happen today. I will be in my bedroom. Do NOT DISTURB."

"I get it," Roberta replied.

So it is about 11:00 a.m., and Ellie is sitting in quiet meditation, waiting for her visit from God. Roberta was at the front desk when a hobo walks in. He was hitchhiking along Route 6, was both stinky and dirty. "I wonder if I could maybe have a sandwich and something to drink," he asks.

Now, Roberta was very sweet and very timid. She also was very dependent on Ellie to make all decisions as it was her motel. So Roberta gently knocked on Ellie's bedroom door. "What is it, Roberta?" She explained about the hobo at the front desk. Ellie was very upset and said, "I asked you not to disturb me. Do we have any leftovers? Give him something and send him on his way."

The door slams, and Ellie continues to wait for the great visitation. All was calm until about 5:00 p.m. A man and his wife pulled up with a station wagon full of children. Roberta could see they were very poor and all in need of baths. The man explained they had been traveling for days and wondered if there was a shower perhaps that had not been cleaned that they could all use.

Poor Roberta, to her, this was big, and she was so timid she decided this was an emergency and knocked on Ellie's door again. This time, Ellie was enraged. "I told you not to bother me. What in the world is it?"

Roberta explained about the family and the father's request.

"Is there a room that has not been cleaned yet?"

"Yes," Roberta replied.

"Then let them use it, and do not bother me again." Ellie spent the entire day until late in the evening, waiting and waiting for her visit from God. At around ten, Ellie whispered to God, "You disappointed me today. You promised you would visit me."

The reply came from deep within her, "No, Ellie, YOU disappointed me. I came two times to see you today. Once you gave me leftovers to eat, and the second time you gave me a dirty shower."

Although Ellie did help these people out, she missed the chance to give God her best. God came to her through these people, and she missed the sign. By staying in her room, it was similar to her having a closed mind. God had simply said, "I will visit you tomorrow, Ellie." He did not say, "Ellie, pray all day."

You don't need to isolate yourself for a visitation from God. In fact, if God is truly in the least, then any person who is helpless and hopeless can be your visitation with God. God can show up no matter where you are. You just might not recognize Him. So now you can see how the family needing a shower was actually God testing Ellie. So was the hobo asking for food. God needed a shower. God needed food. She never came out to greet them.

Open your eyes to see God in everybody. How many times have you seen someone famous walk into a restaurant and get seated right away at their best table? Have you seen it when they show up at a club or a show? They are usually brought to the front of the line. Have you also noticed that a customer may buy a famous athlete their meal? We all have this tendency to give to people who already have. That is the nature of who we are, but the nature of who God is, He would give it to the least. What will you do?

Every child we saved, every life we touched in Romania or any-where, no matter how insignificant, each one was God. Jesus taught this same lesson when He said, "I was sick, and you ministered to Me. I was hungry, and you fed Me. I was in prison, and you visited Me."

They answered Him, "When, Lord, did we visit you in prison, when did we feed you, when were you hungry?"

His answer, "When you did it to the least of these, my brethren, you did it unto Me." No one wants to deal with the least, but when you stoop to help the helpless, God stoops to help you. This is the lesson Ellie gave to me and the reason for my work in Romania.

C H A P T E R   2 4

OshKosh Favor

Although we had approval both in America and Romania, we were not given any children to adopt. "What is the problem?" I remembered asking. Since we did not pay a bribe, the government had wanted us to do something of goodwill for the state orphanages. We had already built a church and an orphanage. We had brought much-needed medicines and antibiotics. We had shipped a whole dental clinic that was donated to us. We had shown that we were honest and cared about the children. There was simply not anything else we could do to earn favor with the Romanian government. We had an office, a great director, a social worker, everything we needed to be an adoption agency, except for one very important thing: children. I was stumped and embarrassed.

A few weeks went by, and one morning, I got a call about a tractor trailer load of OshKosh children's pajamas. It was in Canada, and they wanted to donate it to our work in Romania. If we paid for shipping, they would donate the whole trailer load. I had no idea of the value of this container of pajamas, but I was sure it was quite a lot. We paid for shipping and sent it to Romania. When they received this trailer of brand-new pajamas for the state orphanages, they began to give us these beautiful children.

We now had favor over the next few years, and we were able to place over twenty of these older children into homes in America. I will tell you about a few of them. Many have done well, others had some struggles, but I know they are not here by accident, and each one has a purpose and a destiny.

Salami and Bread, Please

*F*inally, we get the call, and we were informed of a young boy in one of the state orphanages who was available for adoption. We asked if we could take him to our private orphanage in Lipova so he could learn a little English but also just to get him out of that terrible place.

I booked a flight and made arrangements to see him. His name was Alex, but I called him Pisano. He had been abandoned by his mother at the hospital and had been in the orphanage all of his seven years on the earth. It was a disgusting place and was totally inadequate with very poor hygiene. Most dogs have it better in America. We were given permission to take him out for lunch with us. I will never forget how cute he was. He was very excited to be getting parents and even more excited to visit the first McDonalds in the city of Timisoara.

Alex remembers today, when he was seven, playing in the pit of balls in McDonald's. When they asked him what he would like to eat, through the interpreter, he asked for "salami and bread, please." He settled for a Big Mac and a milkshake and was *very* happy. I told him that he'd be able to hit McDonald's with a stone in his new home. He was so excited.

Lecia Frome and Chris Renn were a couple in our church. I talked with them about this little boy. Alex looked so much like Lecia. It was crazy. They agreed they wanted to adopt him. So they went through the process, which took two to three months. When everything was secured, my director, Andy, flew to Romania to bring

Pisano home. Andy told me, "The whole trip, Pisano kept looking out the window, saying, 'America? America?'"

That following Sunday at church, Pisano was in Mama Lecia's arms. The people rejoiced; I wept. All of the adoptions we were able to do were very inexpensive. We were able to work in Romania without paying bribes. The church was paying our social worker and director. Children should never be for sale. It is also not so easy to adopt older children. In his late teens and early twenties, Pisano had some struggles. He never lost his faith in God, and he made his way back to the light.

Today, Pisano is a professional mechanic with a side business of aerial photography. He is married to a beautiful wife, Stacy, and has a beautiful child. As our first orphan adopted, he will always have a special place in my heart.

Recently, he found he has brothers in Romania and also found his biological mother. She was so happy he was alive; she thought he might have been dead. She explained to him that his father was an alcoholic, and when he drank, he was so dangerous. She feared for her life and for his. They were also very poor and had little to eat. She left him at the hospital, and later, when she went back, she could never find where they had placed him. They are all planning to visit soon.

CHAPTER 26

Abandoned Baby

I found Elizabita in a state orphanage. Her mother was fourteen years old and already had two other children. Her father was in prison at the time, and her mother was homeless. The hospital would not let her take the baby, and Elizabita was placed into the state system. The state orphanage she was in was horrible. There were twenty children, all kept in one room. Down the middle was a curtain separating the living and eating area. It was even worse than where I found Pisano. Children were packed into this one room with total inadequate care. I was asked to wait in a small concrete building next to the orphanage. "Please wait here." They were going to bring her to me.

She was pitiful, head shaved bald because of the lice problem. She had one crossed eye and what looked like a clubfoot. She was wearing a little faded sundress and looked so sad. They nudged her, and she sang a little nursery rhyme to me in the sweetest voice. With tears in my eyes, I promised her and myself I would find her a home.

Returning to Pennsylvania, I began my search. There was a couple in my church who had married late in life and did not have children. They were wonderful people, Bob and Jonie Irvine. If you needed something done, these were the people to call. Well, I needed a mom and a dad. I called them and asked if I could drop over and talk to them about something. I told them about Elizabita and showed them the video of her singing. It was as if she was auditioning for parents. With tears of joy from all of us, they agreed, and we began the process. Elizabita was then placed into our own orphanage, Haven of Hope, and soon, Bob and Jonie were on a plane to get their little girl.

At the time, Elizabita was around five years old. This wonderful couple loved her back to life. Her eyes were fixed, and they found her foot was not clubbed, and corrective shoes were the answer. The doctors told us that if her eyes had not been fixed, she would have been blind at some point. When these children come of age, I also know they are turned out into the streets, and many of the girls are sex-trafficked, and the boys become criminals.

Today, Elizabita is married with two beautiful boys and a wonderful husband. My grandsons! She had been searching to see if she could find any information on her family and, amazingly enough, she found them while I was finishing this book. Still, today, they are very poor, and her mother explained to her that she had tried to get her back, but because of her living conditions, she was not allowed to.

Elizabita told her of the incredible life that God had blessed her with. She told of how much she is loved, and they were so happy. Many tears were shed on that FaceTime call. When I see them all on Facebook, it makes me cry, and I always remember, when we do for those who can never do us good in return, God does for us what we cannot do for ourselves.

When We Give

I want to talk about giving. I believe that one dime from every dollar we make does not belong to us. Some call it the tithe. When we separate that tenth of our income, we should find something we believe in and give. Also, above that tenth is the offering that you should give to support those who cannot support themselves. "What?" you say. "Give a tenth and then give more?" Yes!

Many years ago, when I was working for the appraisal company, I had such an opportunity to experience God instructing the universe for me. We were getting ready to build the new church I wrote about previously. It was a Sunday evening in the basement church. We had maybe sixty people at the meeting. My father was talking about the new church that we were going to build and asked if any wanted to give toward the building fund. I did not have it, but for some crazy reason, I pledged $1,000.

The next morning, I went into work. We had finished appraising the whole county, and now people could come in to discuss their new appraisals if they thought they were incorrect. Most of them believed that the appraisal company had made the valuation too high for their property. They would come in and sit across the table from me and discuss why the property is not worth the value.

If it was a home, perhaps the appraiser could not get inside, and we had to make an adjustment as to the condition of the interior. If it was vacant land, many times, it would be about not having egress to the property. It was landlocked. This was the case of one such property. A local attorney owned it. He came into the hearing, sat down across from me, and strange enough, out of seven appraisers working in the county, it was me who had done this appraisal.

It was thirty acres of landlocked land on top of a mountain. I had been very generous, on the low side of the appraisal because I saw that it was landlocked. I believed I had appraised it at $4,000. "This is not worth near that," he stated emphatically.

We were always taught to ask what the owner thought the value should be, so I asked him. "Robert, what do you think the land is worth?"

"Two hundred dollars," was his answer.

"So tomorrow, if I show up at your office," which was right across the street from the courthouse I was working in, "with two hundred dollars, you will sell me that property and give me a deed?"

"Absolutely," he stated.

"Okay," I said. "I will be over in the morning." I was joking, actually, because I knew he would not sell me the thirty acres of land for two hundred dollars.

Later that day, I asked my supervisor if it would be a conflict of interest to buy this land. "Of course not," he said. "But there is no way that attorney is going to sell it for that ridiculous price."

Well, I did not even have two hundred extra dollars at the time, so I borrowed it from my dad, telling him I may be paying him back today as I did not believe the lawyer would sell that land so cheap.

I walked into his office, and his secretary had me take a seat. I thought, *He will be certainly shocked to see me.* Well, he wasn't. He had a quitclaim deed all prepared in my name. I signed a few documents, handed him the two hundred dollars, and quickly walked out of his office. Now, a quitclaim deed is not as good as a general warranty deed for sure. The property could have leans against it or many other problems.

I walked down the street from the attorney's office to the Hammermill Paper Companies office. Stepping inside, I explained to the receptionist that I had these thirty acres of land adjoined by one of their properties, and would they like to purchase it? I gave her a copy of my deed and asked if someone would call if interested.

A few weeks later, I got a call and was asked to come over to the office. I walked in, and they handed me a check for $4,000 for the property. How did this happen? Did the attorney have a brain failure? He could have easily sold the land for more. I believe the moment I made the pledge to give, God made a pledge to be. I paid my father the $200, gave my thousand more to the building fund, and discovered when you give to those who can do you no good, in return, God opens His hand to give to you. Wait, there is more.

A few years ago, I got a phone call from a man who was representing a gas company. They had the rights to drill on the property that was all around the thirty acres I owned for a few weeks. For some crazy reason I did not understand, I held gas and mineral rights to that property. What? How is that possible after all these years? We signed some papers, and he notified me that if they drill a well in that area, I will receive a royalty. Wow. To date, nothing has materialized, but stay tuned!

CHAPTER 28

God's Challenge

As our church was growing in Pennsylvania, we decided it was time to build a larger sanctuary. We had help from other sources for Romania, but the primary support was from our church. We were giving $10,000 per month to Romania, but now we needed those funds to build our new church. But we couldn't stop giving money to Romania. At that time, I was meeting with a few men for two hours, every morning, for meditation and prayer. I knew that it would be impossible to build a new church in America while still supporting Romania.

I remember, early one morning, I felt an overwhelming feeling of faith or even a deep knowing that if we continued to give as we were and also to pray every day, we would build the church and never even have to ask for money.

I remember the day the steel arrived for the new building, four truckloads. The bill for that steel was over $60,000. As the trucks were being unloaded, I knew it would take all the money that was left in our building fund and more. We had already spent much on an architect, excavating, foundation, and all the underground plumbing. All the concrete work was done, and we were ready to put up the steel. In fact, we were short of money, and I was not sure how I was going to pay for the steel. I remember thinking, *I probably should have waited on the steel.* But remember, if you continue to give and stay in prayer, what could happen?

Just as the last truck was being unloaded, a businessman from town pulled into the parking lot of the church. "Is that the steel for the new building?" he asked.

"Yes," I said. "Isn't it wonderful?"

"How much?" he asked.

"A lot," my reply.

"No, really. How much?"

I told him it was $60,000.

Pulling a check out of his pocket, he said, "I knew I would need this today." Taking out his pen, he wrote a check for $60,000.

I cannot tell you how many times that same scenario took place. That beautiful church is finished today. It is state of the art and seats over 1,000 people. We never asked the people to give one time. When we did for those who could not do us any good in return, God did for us what we could not do for ourselves.

CHAPTER 29

Failure

$\mathcal{I}$n 2010, I went through a very painful divorce and felt like a total failure. I stood before my congregation, apologized to them, and left the ministry. I had seen many go through a divorce and continue in ministry, but for me, to continue seemed hypocritical. I had told many who had failed, yes, there is death but also resurrection. I needed my resurrection, and I literally went into hiding and moved to New York State. Though many reached out to me, I did not return their many calls and letters. I was so embarrassed and feeling worthless. How, after I had done so much good, could I end up now a failure? With no fight in me, I gladly accepted whatever terms were in the divorce and tried to move on.

Once in a while, I would see someone from my church who would run up to me and hug me, but every time, I felt so sad that I had let them down. You are not your failures, and neither was I. When you're in the middle of the muddy mess, it's hard to comprehend a way out. It was crazy waking up every morning to such a drastic change. If I ever needed God, it was now. One thing for sure is this: even if you give up on you, He never will. He has never changed the plan for my life. In fact, every failure we will ever make, He knew, and He has a blueprint for your path. If you could see it, you would see you are in the perfect place, though uncomfortable, for your divine encounter. I began to remember the call on my life, and you should too. Why? Because everyone has a purpose, and because you have a purpose, He has a plan for you. In spite of you and me, our purpose will become our reality if we do not quit.

As mine, your experience must be shared with others, even if it may be difficult because without your story, someone may not be able to write theirs. As I said in the beginning and throughout this book, it's not because of me but in spite of me. God has not changed His mind about who I really am. I, like Gideon, am a mighty man. When we take responsibility for our failures, God takes responsibility for our successes. That's why I went to my church on a Sunday morning and gave them an apology. It was difficult to do but a cleansing of the soul.

Here I want to personally thank Jason Holmberg who, for the past ten years, has continued the ministry in Romania. While I was in my darkest hour, he continued to travel to Romania. His investment, both financially and with his own time, he gave freely to continue what I had started. I can never thank him enough. I also want to thank his father, Jeffrey Holmberg, who traveled to Romania with a team to build and bless Romania.

C H A P T E R   3 0

Why Me? Why Not You?

If you remember, in the beginning, I wrote about Gideon from the Old Testament, Judges, the sixth chapter. When this angel appeared to Gideon, he was hiding from his enemies. The angel salutes Gideon and says two things that we should talk about. First, he tells him that God is with him, and second, he is a mighty man of valor. I love the honest response of Gideon. "If God is with us, then why has all of this befallen us?"

He says, "God IS with us." If God is with us, and it's this bad, can you imagine how bad it would be if God wasn't with us? It would be much worse.

"And, by the way, where are all the miracles we used to hear about? And, as for a mighty man," Gideon continued, "of all the clans, mine is the least, of all the families in that clan, mine is the least, and of all the people in my family, I am the least."

This is a guy with a great problem with his own self-worth and abilities. He had allowed his environment to determine who he was. We all do this. If all is at peace around us, and we have enough, all is well. But when our world is rocked, we become someone else. We are sometimes even shocked at who we become. When the angel greets Gideon, he greets him as who he really is, not as he sees himself.

The environment you are in, which affects you, even at your worst, is not you. You may be hiding or freaking out, but that is not who you are. Others will agree that you are a mess, but that is not who you are. You may look at the success of others and say, "I am the least." When you do, your environment is moving to a path that

74

is not you. I am sure you have heard the saying, "God doesn't use perfect people." What that really means is that there are not any! If there were, it would certainly make sense to use them. So he has no choice to use the imperfect Gideons of the earth. The you and me.

As for Gideon, do you think he felt totally incapable? You bet he did. Did he have his moments of fear? All the time! He asked five times, in many crazy ways, to be sure! I think if an angel visited me, I might believe. But not Gideon. He was so sure he was the wrong choice based on his opinion of who he thought he was. If you read the whole story, when Gideon finally pulls an army together to battle, this invading army had 32,000 men going up against a number they could not count. Then God tells him to send anyone home who is afraid.

Twenty-two thousand took the deal and left. I would have gladly joined them. Then, just before the battle was to begin, another test, and all but 300 were sent home. Why? Because it can never be because of us; it will always be in spite of us, at least if we are honest.

A few hours later, as mass hysteria swept over the enemy camp below, and without Gideon raising a weapon, God delivered Israel. We all have a dream, a vision, a calling, an idea. Did you ever think this would be a great idea if it would have been given to someone smarter than you? Every time I encountered problems, I would begin this thought. But you now must know what I have come to know, that the vision or idea or whatever it is that has come to you was put in front of *you*. Listen to the voice that says you're mighty, you're powerful, you're not the least. Don't look back at yesterday's mistakes or failures. Remember, your focus will become your future. If you focus on the past, it will become your future. Some live a life that is the past over and over again.

Think about the windshield in your car. It is very large, allowing you a good view of what is in front of you. The rearview mirror, however, is small, allowing you to look back as only a reference. Don't try it, but it is impossible to safely operate your car if you are looking where you have been instead of where you are going. More than a glance will derail or even destroy your future. You are not your past environment or your present. You, like Gideon, are a great man or woman of valor. No one may believe it, not even you. Gideon didn't. As I am writing this book, I am reminded of how totally incapable I felt, how so afraid I was, so many times. No hero here. But to God, you're a mighty man. Your dream does not terminate because of you. Even if you give up on it, God never gives up on you.

I am reminded of Reverend Elias Koteta. Elias traveled with me a few times to Romania and, once, I with him to Lebanon. He shared his story with me. Elias was born in Lebanon and actually played for the national basketball team from Lebanon. His dream was to come to California because he said he wanted to see the beaches and bikinis! He planned to come to America then, find some woman to marry him, which should not be a problem because he was very handsome, then he would divorce her and have his papers to stay. He enrolled in college and was looking for a job.

Years before this, there was a little girl in Sunbury, Pennsylvania. Her name was Sandy. She was playing in the park, and she had a vision. In this vision, God told her, "I am going to show you your husband." She saw his face and noticed it was of dark complexion, and God said, "He will be from the Middle East and, together, you will do great things for me."

Years later, Sandy is married to a man with whom she had become pregnant, a professional musician who had dreams of moving to California and becoming part of the Beach Boys. He did have the opportunity to play with the Beach Boys for a short while. Now, with two children, she moved with him to California, where he abandoned her and their children, and she was alone. She later told me she knew she had missed that great event of meeting her true love. For her, it was over, but for God, He is busy working.

She reconnected with a good church, began to help others, and was blessed with a job managing a restaurant. And guess who came in for an interview? Elias. When she saw him, she knew who he was. This was the man she saw as a little girl in the park! He was standing right in front of her, asking for a job!

When Elias saw that she had an interest in him, he immediately asked her out, and they soon married. He was not interested in being with her, he told me. "I did not love her and just was biding my time." Every Sunday, Sandy would ask Elias if he would attend church with her. His answer was always no.

One morning, she came down for church, and he was sitting on the couch with his suit on. "I have decided to go one time, just to shut your mouth," he told her. Elias told me how he sat in the back, and when the music began to play, something began to happen to his heart. He told me how he began to weep and shake. He ran to the front of that church and said, "God, if you're real, then let me love my wife." He told me, when he looked at her with tear-filled eyes, "David, I fell madly in love with Sandy." They traveled the world together for over thirty years.

If ever you think you were late or you have totally missed it, if you have a dream, a calling, a purpose, something in your heart that would help others, then try this: do good to those who can never do you good in return and see if God will not instruct the universe to work for you, what you cannot do for yourself. *He* can and *He* will.

C H A P T E R 3 1

Argument versus Experience

I am not a man with an argument as to the existence of God. Many have that argument; I've had an experience. You just read it. My dear grandmother did not find God in a traditional church. She found Him out of desperation in a little storefront with a handful of Black ladies. She did not have an argument about whether or not God existed. She had an experience. She had a total encounter with the God of the universe, and her faith was unmovable. That experience caused her to have a great love for people. There was no judgment in my grandmother. No matter where you came from or who you were, all were welcome at her table. She made God personal for everyone. Through Christ, she taught of His mercy and grace for all, even those who the world rejected.

From the high to the low, she shared her amazing faith. She taught that all were deserving of this personal experience with a living God. For some reason, she had a real love for Jewish people. Many doctors in New York were Jewish. She would make an appointment for a checkup, and after the doctor would be finished with her checkup, she gently began to talk to them about God. You could write a book on the many lives she touched. She had such a way of speaking with that Southern drawl that people were moved by her words and the genuine love from her heart.

After she moved to Pennsylvania, once every couple of years, she would visit family in Tennessee. She also took many trips to Florida during the winter. My cousin, Jim, recounted one such trip. Grandmother never drove over forty-five miles per hour, not ever. As she would travel, she would have to get on interstates and highways that require minimum speeds. She had been pulled over quite a few times for going too slow. She was always very polite and was quick to hand the officers her insurance and registration papers. This time, the policeman gave her a short lecture to speed it up a little. When he was done and giving her back her papers, she asked him if she had interfered in any way with him doing his job. "No, ma'am," he said, "you have been very cooperative."

"Well, now, please allow me to do my job," she replied. She began to talk to him about God and how He had a plan for him and that everything was going to be okay. She read his mail, so to speak. Tears were flowing down his face from behind his sunglasses. When she said, let's pray, he lifted both hands over his head. To a passerby, it looked as if he was being held up. I cannot imagine what his superior officer would have thought if he had driven up on the scene!

My aunt recounted to me another trip. As they were driving down the highway, somewhere in the South, my grandmother came upon a chain gang. These were men chained together and forced to work for their crimes. It was common, at that time, especially in the South, and it was quite brutal in the hot summer sun. My dear grandmother stopped her Rambler, remember those? Then she walked up to the guards. "I am a minister," she said, "and I want to talk to these boys about their souls."

"Ma'am, these boys are hardened criminals. That one over there is a murderer, that one tried to kill his own brother, and that one is a rapist. These boys don't care nothing about God," the guard replied.

My aunt recalled to me how Grandma convinced the guards to let her speak to these men. Sitting them all down, she began to speak to them. She told them that God loved them and that He would forgive them, and soon tears were falling from their faces as she spoke to them. Then she gathered them together, and they prayed. What good could these desperate men ever do my grandmother? None. But when you do for those who cannot do you any good in return, God does for you what you cannot do for yourself. Sometimes, even in spite of you!

CHAPTER 32

Haven of Hope Today

*T*oday, the Haven of Hope Orphanage is doing well. Support comes from a couple of sources, but for Pastor Moses, it was his goal to become as self-sufficient as possible. Pastor Moses built a huge greenhouse, and much of the food for the children is grown there. For meat, they raise their own turkeys as well as chickens and pigs. Many of the children have gone on to college and tech schools. They have married, and some still attend the church in Lipova. Recently, Pastor Moses has purchased ostriches, which is a very popular source of protein in Romania.

What I Learned from a Little Jewish Girl

*A*fter my divorce, I was living in New York. My son, Jesse, and his wife, Tracy, along with my two grandchildren, had moved to Sarasota, Florida. I wanted to be close to them, so I was thinking about, perhaps, moving south. I was ready to shuck the shovel, and if I never saw snow again, that would be all right! A friend of mine, a local professor, had met a wonderful lady, and they began to date. "How did you meet?" I asked.

"Online."

"Online?" I had heard crazy stories of online dating and wanted no part of it up until now. Finding the only free site, Plenty of Fish, I went online and signed up! I read an intriguing post from a lady in Sarasota. She stated, "I am not religious, but I am spiritual." That is the same thing my grandmother used to say. So I thought, *Why not?* And I reached out to her.

Her name was Michele. I explained I was thinking of moving to Florida and asked her what she meant about being spiritual. She shared her life with me, and I shared mine with her. She had forgiven some things that were done to her that most would not have. She had learned to let go of blame and guilt. She told me how she was free from a life of unforgiveness. We talked, every night, for hours. I have never in my life talked so much for so long to anyone. We talked about God, what it meant to be spiritual, and then she told me about her book. She had created this book, with two *New York*

Times best-selling authors, with her simple yet immovable faith. It was called *Peace in the Present Moment*. At that time, it had not been published but was to be released soon. Michele had been given Eckhart Tolle's book *The Power of Now* as a gift. This is a book about present moment awareness, forgiveness, and letting go of the past and yesterday's guilt.

She began a life of gratitude and discovered a strength in herself that she didn't know existed. She said that flowers grabbed her attention for some reason, their inner beauty captivated her, and she had an intense desire to capture that moment for others. She photographed flowers from a different perspective. She got really close to the inside of the flower to photograph those tiny hairs, little wisps, and vibrant colors. She called them her "soul shots." They brought her a peace she had not known before. If you remember, Jesus taught His disciples to consider the lilies, and how they did not toil or worry about tomorrow.

In his book, Eckhart writes, "seeing beauty in a flower could awaken humans, however briefly, to the beauty that is an essential part of their own innermost being, their true nature." She placed some of her photographs in local art shows and won awards. Her photographs were spectacular. While meditating, she had what she called "an inspired thought." The world needs a book of flowers to meditate on along with quotes from Eckhart Tolle's book. She imagined what it would look like. She really felt it as if it were done. She always says, "If you believe it and feel it, then you can become it."

Then she created a mock-up book with her floral photographs and his quotes and had it bound together. She began to tell every one of her soon coming book with this *New York Times* best-selling author. Literally, everyone she came in contact with. She spoke as if it were already done. There wasn't any doubt in her mind that this would come to be.

How does a no-name photographer get a *New York Times* best-selling author to collaborate on a book? Everyone told her that if Eckhart Tolle wanted a book with flowers and his quotes, he would, more than likely, choose a famous photographer from *National Geographic*. No one thought it was possible; in fact, it wasn't. In faith, she began to imagine how she would feel walking through the airport and seeing the book for sale. She imagined the phone call she would be getting, telling her the book is now in production. She imagined meeting Eckhart and talking about their book together. She had quite the imagination. Really, she had great faith, and unknown to her, that inspired thought came from a divine source.

Through a series of events that could only be the universe under the direction of a mighty God, she attended a Louise Hay conference in Tampa, Florida. There, she ordered a large candle from one of the vendors. When the candle arrived at her home a few days later, it was the wrong color. She called the lady from whom she had purchased it, and she agreed to send her the correct color, and then they talked for a bit. "Everything happens for a reason," the woman said.

Michele agreed with her but couldn't imagine what this reason could be. As she told everyone, Michele told Lori about her plans to have a book with Eckhart Tolle. Lori told her that she had published a book, *A Victim No More*, and that her publisher, Bob Friedman of Hampton Roads Publishing, had just completed a children's book with Eckhart Tolle. Lori was so inspired by Michele's story and idea that she offered to call Bob Friedman and tell him about her idea. Bob agreed to receive an email from Michele. She was to keep it short and sweet as the publisher had a pile of manuscripts from floor to ceiling to review for that month alone, and he was doing this as a favor to Lori.

Not long after sending her proposal to him, he replied to her. He loved the idea, but he didn't think it would be possible to collaborate with Eckhart Tolle. Michele told Bob she knew if Eckhart could see her work, he would feel the same inspiration and passion she felt when reading his words. Her photographs were full of passion, inspiration, healing, and presence, and she believed Eckhart would connect with them deep to his soul.

Bob asked her to send him the mock-up book, but instead, she jumped on a plane and headed to Virginia. She wanted to see his face when he opened the book. It was worth it. The look on Bob's face was priceless. He loved the book and called in the CEO and marketing director at Hampton Roads, and they loved it too. They had other writers they wanted to connect her with, such as Neale Donald Walsh, who had written *Conversations with God*, another *New York Times* best-seller, but she insisted they must get it to Eckhart.

She stuck to her inspired thought. She was so determined that they agreed to send the mock-up book to Eckhart's publisher, Namaste, in Canada. If Namaste liked it, then and only then would the book be given to Eckhart personally. She didn't question whether Eckhart would get to see it or whether he would like it because she *knew*.

Months went by, and she continued to keep the feeling; it is already done. One day, while shopping at Best Buy, she got a call from Bob Friedman. He said, "Are you sitting down?"

With nowhere to sit, she says, "No, but please continue."

Bob continued. "Because of your genuine spirit, passion, and belief, Namaste loved your book and has agreed to show it to Eckhart."

Well, Eckhart loved the book, too, and even brought in a second *New York Times* best-selling author, Byron Katie, to collaborate with. In October of 2010, *Peace in the Present Moment* was published and released. Jack Canfield's first book, *Chicken Soup for the Soul,* was rejected by 144 publishers. How did Michele get three yesses? One from Hampton Roads, one from Namaste, and one from Eckhart Tolle. Now that little Jewish girl had some kind of faith.

We talked on the phone for eight weeks before we ever met. I could not upload pictures very well and had learned that the pictures some people post of themselves are not accurate, to put it politely. If her picture was even close to what she actually looked like, I was good, as she was such an amazing person. I flew to Tampa, rented a car, and agreed to meet her at Marina Jack's in Florida. It had been months of only conversation, and I was a bit nervous. Marina Jack's is a beautiful place right on Sarasota Bay.

When I arrived at Marina Jack's, I saw her sitting at a table waiting for me. She was beautiful, in every way, and I was so happy. We had a bite to eat, and then we held hands and took a walk in the park, right next to the restaurant. It was in that same park I would ask her to be mine forever, a few months later. I kissed her for the first time, and it was wonderful. It was like fireworks going off in my head.

Still living in New York, we continued the long-distance dating. It's not fun, but it sure makes you appreciate the time you get to be together. She was so amazing and so sweet; I thought for sure this is too perfect. We had been dating a few months when, one evening, we were going out to dinner. We were walking down the street, and I prayed to myself, "God, please show me if this is the one." She was perfect, but everyone is in the beginning. Surely, there is another shoe to drop. So I simply said to God, "Please give me a sign. A big one, though, because sometimes, I am blind. Did you send Michele here for me to spend the rest of my life with?"

At that moment, as we are walking to dinner, we had to pass a casino that was located just before the restaurant, one of the slot machines hits, and it is dinging *very* loudly. It got our attention, and when we looked at it, it was flashing my last name in huge lights, Minor, then the number 33 repeatedly. After the woman collected her jackpot and continued to play, we watched as the numbers on the top of the machine would go from minor to major numbers and, at that very moment I was walking by, it hit on Minor 33. So is that the sign? Or is it just coincidence?

Minor was definitely the sign, but what did the *33* mean? It's part of the sign. Not quite convinced because we needed to know what the *33* meant. I took Michele's hand and said, "Come with me."

We walked into the casino, and I found the roulette wheel. You had to sit to play, so I sat Michele down, bought one chip, and placed it on the number 33. I decided that we would put one chip on the number 33, and with *one* spin, if it hits, then she's the one. Crazy, right? Well, one spin, I closed my eyes, and then I heard Michele start to scream. When I opened my eyes, the marble had landed on the number 33! Yes, I even asked the man if anyone had moved the marble. His answer, "No one touches the marble, sir."

Yes, someone did that day. God is ever in charge! Enough already; she is the one. It was the best decision that someone else ever made for me. Thirty-three is now our number! It appeared every-where we went. When I moved to Florida, they gave me a new phone number. When I added the numbers together, they added up to thirty-three. We saw 33 on license plates, on buildings, on mile markers, the final tab of our bill, and much more. A few months after getting my sign, we took our vows on a beach in Puerto Rico, under an arbor of beautiful flowers that had, for some reason, been left on the beach from a previous wedding.

Today, she has a ministry of making mats for the homeless to sleep on. It is called Bags to Beds. She takes the recycled plastic bags from local markets and cuts them into plarn (plastic yarn) and then crochets them into mats to keep the homeless off the wet ground. It takes over 600 bags to make one mat. When she has finished, she takes them to the homeless downtown. She says, "If we can't get them off the street, we can at least get them off the ground." She is doing good for those who can never do her good in return. I am so proud of her, and I am blessed to wake up to this beautiful and wonderful woman every day, Michele, my love.

EPILOGUE

This book was not written in any way to make me out to be a special person. I am not. I am just like everyone else with flaws, failures, and disappointments. The message I hope you receive is that God sees you differently than you see yourself. When you have a dream or a vision, and you know that vision would help people, then pursue it. Just take the first step, like trademark the name or open a bank account in the name of the new business or even clearly write it down in detail. In the Old Testament, Habakkuk is told to write the vision and make it plain. That alone is a step of faith.

You must begin to believe in yourself and realize that God believes in you. Focus on your future. And remember, if you focus on the past, it will manifest itself in the future. Changing the way you think about every situation you are in allows you to get a God view. Because He sees the end at the beginning, you must know that even if you feel like life has put you on a detour, sometimes by your own making, God still sees you victorious at the end of the journey. For a while, I was the man off course, but God never changed His mind about who David really was—an imperfect man with a perfect God, who did great things, in spite of me.

About the Author

David Minor is an ordinary man. As a young sixteen-year-old boy, his grandmother, a most amazing woman who loved God and people, had a conversation with David. "I was not given a choice," David explains. "It was either answer the call of God or there would be no reason for Him to keep me on the earth." Reluctantly, David answered that call. "I didn't enlist," he proclaimed. "I was drafted."

There is great comfort in knowing it was God's idea. This is his story of miracles and the amazing feats that can be accomplished in spite of you. From fear to faith, you will understand that God can do much, not because of you but in spite of you.

From building churches and orphanages in Romania, an adoption agency to rescue the children, dangerous, impossible border crossing, and much more, you will not be able to put this book down.